THE PARISH: EUCHARISTIC COMMUNITY

CASIANO FLORISTAN

The Parish: Eucharistic Community

Translated by JOHN F. BYRNE
with a Foreword by LOUIS J. PUTZ, C.S.C.

SHEED AND WARD
LONDON AND MELBOURNE

FIRST PUBLISHED IN GREAT BRITAIN IN 1965
SHEED AND WARD LTD
33 MAIDEN LANE
LONDON W.C.2
AND
SHEED AND WARD PTY LTD
28 BOURKE STREET
MELBOURNE

Originally published as *La Parroquia, Communidad Eucaristica,* Madrid, Ediciones Marova, S.L. (1961)

NIHIL OBSTAT: LOUIS J. PUTZ, C.S.C.
University of Notre Dame

IMPRIMATUR: LEO A. PURSLEY, D.D.
Bishop of Fort Wayne-South Bend

Printed in Great Britain by
Lowe & Brydone (Printers) Ltd., London

DEDICATION

To my mother, who is at rest in the Lord.
To my mother parish at Arguedas.

FOREWORD
TO THE ENGLISH EDITION

Since the call of Pope John toward an *aggiornamento,* a bringing of the Church up to date to meet the man of the twentieth century and answer his need for God and salvation, the Church has not been the same. It is not that the Church has changed in its divinely appointed mission, or that the structure of the Church needs overhauling. It is society that has changed and the Church must meet the new man who is the product of this society. This man has become adult and mature because he is educated. His place in the Church will have to be recognized if the Church is going to have relevance for him. He must be approached in a quite different way than formerly.

Society is not predominantly rural any more. Modern

man is urban. Transportation and modern means of communication have brought the city even into the rural areas. Industrialization has changed society completely and the work of science is going to accomplish a still greater transformation of modern society. The Church, especially in its basic unit, the local parish, will have to make major adaptations. More than any other part of the Church structure, the parish will feel the effects of these new conditions for the Church. Liturgical reform will make its greatest impact in the local community of the parish. The work of education, especially adult education in religious responsibility will again fall on the parochial clergy if it is going to reach the great mass of the modern population. And where will apostolic men, conscious of their full membership in the Church, conscious of their role to bear witness to Christ and the Christian way of life, conscious of the influence that they will have to exert on modern society, get their daily encouragement and their daily strengthening if not at the altar and through the ministration of the local parish?

When it is a question of changing anything, then it is important that those who envisage necessary changes have a firm footing from which to proceed. This is the importance of this book. Its author is Spanish, but he relies almost exclusively on the rethinking and restructuring that have been going on in Germany and France and to some extent in other countries in an effort to bring the Church to meet the challenge of modern times. In this country the Church has been strongly influenced by the need for parochial schools. At this moment we are beginning to realize that we shall never be able to accommodate all our children in Catholic schools. We are beginning to take into account the vast majority of children who frequent public elementary and secondary schools. We are also becoming aware of the adult need to grow in religious knowledge as one becomes more and more expert in the secular field, and especially as one becomes aware that he must be a front-line apostle for the Church.

It is vitally important that we know the history and theology of Church organization. It is important that we know where to go to discover a theology of parish life and parish activity. This is the burden of the present volume. If it does nothing else but make us more sure of our base of operation, it will have rendered an inestimable service. Change we all must, if the world is not going to bypass the Church. The insecurity and tension felt by most of us result from the attempt to distinguish the essentials that cannot be changed from the principle of change that we can work with. This book acquaints us at least with the past; we must learn to chart the future of the parish, especially the American parish.

Louis J. Putz, C.S.C.
University of Notre Dame

CONTENTS

INTRODUCTION

It may be said that pastoral theology, with the accent on "pastoral," is a fairly recent discovery in the world of the ecclesiastical sciences. Needless to say, the *cura animarum* dates back much farther, to the beginnings of the Church herself and even earlier, since it already existed in some form in the religious life of Yahweh's people.

Action in man precedes reflection. Thus, religion came before theology and the care of souls came before pastoral theology. As a result, we sometimes hear people say that what matters is a religious life and the practice of charity. This is quite true: the most important thing is indeed to live a religious life and practice charity. But this does not mean we can dismiss reflection, which has its own important role. The history of the Church, beginning with the Bible and continuing right on down to the present day, demonstrates that contemplation is absolutely essential to Christianity. While it is true that Christianity is basically a way of life, at the same time it cannot be denied that it is also a doctrine.

"God, who at sundry times and in divers manners spoke in times past to the fathers by the prophets, last of all in these days has spoken to us by his Son" (Heb. 1:1-2). Is it possible to speak to man without words? Can one believe something without hearing it? And can one hear without a minimum of thought? We do not pretend that reflection is the essential element, but rather that in some fashion it must accompany man's life. The *cura animarum*, which is a life of charity, must be nourished by an authentic pastoral theology. What matters, certainly, is the life of the soul, but how can we come to know that life?

Two kinds of difficulties immediately come to mind in relation to pastoral theology. On the one hand, some theologians, who are themselves naturally very fond of reflection, consider that pastoral theology is not a theology at all but a practice, and as such does not qualify as a science. They only admit a *cura animarum* to the lowest and most prosaic plane, where they feel practical things belong. What does theology mean to them? They will say it is a science of God and things, of God in the light of revelation. And is the care of souls not one of the things of God? Did Christ not become man *propter nostram salutem?* Is the Church not the Mystical Body of Christ? Do the Gospels not end with the sending forth of the Apostles into the world, which is God's domain? The first fundamental of pastoral thought ought to come from theology. And if some theologians do not consider pastoral theology as a theological or scientific discipline, they must at least admit, if they are conscientious, that the scientific theology that they teach ought to bear a profoundly pastoral stamp. In any event, it will be possible to discuss the existence of a pastoral theology when it is recognized that all of theology is pastoral.

The second difficulty proceeds from pastors, although it is very like the first. "Nothing is so useless for revitalizing a more or less fossilized reality," it has been written, "as to come with literature and theorems to men who, after all, have the benefit of practical experience."[1] Why do Paul's epistles to particular communities, designed to solve sometimes grave problems, begin with something similar to what the aforementioned author calls "literature and theorems"? It is absolutely necessary to return to the New Testament in order to establish pastoral criteria. Some priests engaged in the pastoral ministry, clearly not very deep thinkers, clamor for concrete and practical remedies, tried and proven formulas, recipes to solve each and every one of their problems. Anyone trying to supply such remedies must rise to the level of revelation in order to avoid the danger of falling into an unprincipled pragmatism, which is perhaps even worse than theological reflection which lacks a thorough pastoral orientation.

Unfortunately for pastoral matters, the patristic era is over. Besides being saints and theologians, the Fathers were also pastors—shepherds of souls—and most of them were bishops. It is not merely a coincidence that the letter which a bishop writes to the members of his diocese should be called a "pastoral" letter. Actually, pastoral theology ought to be written only by shepherds of God's flock.

God grant that the time come soon when pastors

1 Cf. *Comunidad cristiana parroquial* (Madrid: Euramérica, 1959), p. 534.

write theologically and theologians write pastorally. There are indeed wonderful exceptions, but pastoral literature is still a long way from a modern patristics conversant with scholastic theology, or a great modern scholasticism fed from the eternal spring of patristics.

Since one always has to begin with the Bible, it is there that we begin this study of the parish, the special field where the Church's normal pastoral activity takes place. From the Bible we shall go next to history, not with mere passing curiosity but rather with the radical conviction that divine salvation is intimately linked to the *kairoi* of history. Once we have been able to cast some light on the subject through these first two chapters of positive theology, we shall view the parish according to the principles of speculative theology. The universal Church will be considered first, passing afterwards to the diocese or local Church, since in the final analysis the theology of the parish is based on a theology of the Church.

The purpose of this book is without a doubt ambitious. Theologians will perhaps find inaccuracies or a lack of connection in the over-all work. Pastors may feel that it is merely one more work of theory. In order to write really well about the parish, we realize, it would be necessary to add a great pastoral experience such as the Fathers had to a clear and well-founded theology such as the great scholastics had.

In any event, this book is an attempt. If it manages to stir up a little interest in some theologian or pastor, thereby assisting in the building up of the Mystical Body of Christ, the author's difficulties in writing it will be more than compensated.

CHAPTER ONE

THE PARISH IN THE BIBLE

1. In the Old Testament

a) Origin of the word

Very often the etymological study of a concept which corresponds to an important historical reality can shed much light, not only helping us to know the history of the concept's evolution, but also to understand more broadly its current meaning. In the case of the concept we have today of the parish, this study is indispensable.

The word "parish" (in Latin "paroecia" or "parochia") comes from the Greek word "paroikía." Even earlier than this is the word "paroikós," which in the classical writers such as Herodotus, Aeschylus, Sophocles and Thucydides means "neighbor."[1] Likewise, the word "paroikós" was commonly used as a synonym for "foreigner," a resident in a country and with certain rights to protection by the community but without citizenship. The verb "paroikein," like the noun, means "to

1 K. L. & M. A. Schmidt, πάροιχος, παροιχία, παροιχέω, in G. Kittel, *Theol. Wörterbuch zum NT*, V (1954), 840.

live together" on the one hand and "to live abroad" without right of citizenship, on the other.

Biblical Greek began to use the word "paroikía," derived from the earlier concepts. "Paroikein" in the Septuagint means "to live in a foreign country," and "paroikós" is the foreigner who lives in a community where he enjoys some privileges, but without full citizenship. Thus Abraham was a foreigner or *parochial* in Egypt (Gen. 12:10), in Palestine (Gen. 21:34), in Chanaan (Gen. 17:8); Lot was one in Sodom (Gen. 19:9), Isaac in Chanaan (Gen. 26:3) and in Egypt Jacob's sons formed a *paroikía.*

Since the time of Abraham the Hebrews have preserved a religious awareness of being *foreigners* in a world which is not theirs; they form a *parish,* that is to say, a community on pilgrimage toward the Promised Land. The biblical origin of the term "parish" is neither juridical nor sociological but purely and simply religious.

b) The Hebrew community

What was the religious character of the primitive Hebrew community? We would undoubtedly stray far from the objective of this book were we to analyze this important problem too closely, but in order to be really Christian, the parish community ought to be heir to the principal characteristics of the Chosen People.

It has already been seen that the word "parish," although of Greek origin grammatically, finds its deepest religious meaning in the Hebrew mentality.

Abraham is our Father (Rom. 4:11) by virtue of having founded the first assembly of believers. God called him, demanding of him a total uprooting from the land where he had lived (Gen. 12:1-5). He made a pact with God, who required of him an unconditional faith, promising him in return that his descendants would be innumerable (Gen. 15:1-18). The calling, promise, and covenant of God with Abraham are valid for all his descendants, among whom are numbered not only the sons by circumcision but also those sealed by Baptism. "I will make you exceedingly fruitful; I will make nations of you, and kings shall descend from you. I will establish my covenant between you and me and your descendants after you throughout their generations, as a perpetual covenant, that I may be a God to you and to your descendants after you. I will give you and your descendants after you this land in which you are immigrants, all the land of Chanaan as a perpetual possession; and I will be their God" (Gen. 17: 6-8).

Abraham began the great pilgrimage of the Jewish people. God promised him a land, the symbol of a definitive Land. He and his people would always be foreign dwellers; they were to form a *parish*, that is to say, a community of pilgrims living in a borrowed land.

To form part of this Hebrew community of foreigners it was necessary to join the Covenant through faith. It was not enough to receive the seal of circumcision. This rite of matrimonial fertility is a sign of the promise of fertility contained in the Covenant. What matters is circumcision of the heart (Rom. 2:28-29 and 4:9-12).

The Israelites formed a real *parish* in Egypt. While living as slaves in the midst of a pagan people, they nevertheless remained faithful to the Covenant, desiring to continue their pilgrimage to the Promised Land. Moses was the liberator who was to organize the Jewish *parish* in the great exodus of the Hebrews from Egypt to the Promised Land through the Red Sea (Jewish Baptism), a passage ritualized for all time with the supper of the Jewish lamb (Hebrew Passover).

The temptation of the Jewish people consisted in

turning back toward Egypt, in opposing the spiritual meaning of the holy pilgrimage.

The Hebrew, when he ceases to be a pilgrim and becomes a citizen of the world, betrays the promise God made to Abraham. In order that this promise be fulfilled God stirred up vocations, and guarded in a special way a holy Remnant, the Remnant of Israel. The Remnant carried within it the profound sense of *paroikein,* of sojourn. It constituted a *new people,* formed by the pilgrims, or *paroikoi,* who followed the path toward a New Land. The Remnant is not the residue of a generation, but the seed of a new future.

From one Remnant to another, God continued to keep His promises to set up the true *paroikía* of Israel despite human failings. Jesus Christ would concentrate within Himself all the holy Remnant; He was to be the Servant of Yahweh, the Just Man who escaped the general condemnation, the definitive seed of the New People, the authentic *paroikós* of the messianic community. All who believe in Him and baptize themselves in Him with the new circumcision of the Holy Spirit in their hearts form the true *paroikía* of God.

Along with the notion of parish there is yet another which is developed at great length in the Old Testament: it is the concept of *assembly* (in Hebrew *qahal* and in Greek *ekklesía*).

The first characteristic of the Jewish assembly was the fact that it was a *convocation,* decided by the supreme authority of the people in the name of God (Cf. 3 Kings 8:1-2; 2 Par. 15:8-10; 30; etc.).

The assembly that had been gathered together listened to the Word of God (Deut. 31:10-12; 4 Kings 23; 2 Esd. 8, 9; etc.) which ended with an explanation of this Word (3 Kings 8:21; 4 Kings 8:7-8). The purpose of the reading and commentary was to stir up in the people a profession of faith (Deut. 27:14-26).

But the word was always sealed with a religious action; thus we find the sacrificial rite which was carried out in the assembly and which was joined to the prayer of the celebrant or presiding official in the form of a blessing or thanksgiving. This prayer, together with the profession of faith and the rite, constituted the assembly's response to the word of God (3 Kings 8:22-60).

The assembly finally ended with a dismissal, which was normally performed by the presiding official (3 Kings 8:66; Jos. 24:28; 2 Par. 7-10).

The Jewish assembly is a figure of the future universal assembly. In the fullness of time the concept of *paroikía* and of *ekklesía* would be reunited. Christ was the one who would call together the new assembly, the universal parish.[2]

2. In the New Testament

a) The Christian community

In the New Testament, that words "paroikós" (Acts 7:6; Eph. 2:19; 1 Pet. 1:17; 2:11) and "paroikía" (Acts 13:17) and "paroikein" (Luke 24:18; Heb. 11:9) appear with the same biblical sense we have just seen in quotations from the Old Testament as well as from texts closely related to it.[3]

Speaking of the importance of faith in the life of the Patriarchs, Paul declares that Abraham, "By faith . . .

2 Cf. articles by Martimort on the "assembly" in *La Maison-Dieu,* Nos. XX, XLI, LVII, and LX. Also see J. Hild, "Le mystère de la célébration," *La Maison-Dieu,* XX, pp. 83-113 and R. Gantoy, "La asamblea en la economía de la salvation," *Asambleas del Señor,* I, 56-82.

3 F.-X. Arnold, *Glaubensverkündigung und Glaubensgemeinschaft* (Düsseldorf: 1955), p. 76.

abode in the Land of Promise as in a foreign land, dwelling in tents with Isaac and Jacob, the co-heirs of the same promise" (Heb. 11:9). And Peter advises the first Christians: "Conduct yourselves with fear in the time of your sojourning" (1 Pet. 1:17).

All through the Bible, pilgrimages have a great importance. Begun by David, the practice reached its apex with Solomon, when the Ark of the Covenant was carried to the Temple.

The Jewish people's goal of reaching Sion caused their incessant pilgrimage. When the Ark was at last deposited in the Temple, they would be able to rest. Meanwhile, they formed the *paroikía* of God.

The Jews' exilic rite par excellence was their pilgrimage to Jerusalem. In truth they are strangers in every nation around the world. Their real homeland, toward which they travel in a *parish* way, is the holy city of Jerusalem.

Christ also made two solemn pilgrimages to Jerusalem as the Gospels tell us: in the first He passed along the way unnoticed when He went to be presented in the Temple (Luke 2:22-51), and in the last He was joyously acclaimed (Luke 19:28-38) during the triumphal procession of palms. Jesus' ministry is presented by the Evangelists as a going up of the Lord to Jerusalem, the final time this is done being especially stressed (Matt. 20:17-19).

However, Christ completed His sojourn—His Passover among us—with His definitive ascension to the heavenly Jerusalem.

Christ's humanity, first carnal and then mystical, was to be the spiritualized Jerusalem. The Church is now the earthly Jerusalem since it is the Mystical Body of Christ. We Christians are sojourners in the world—true strangers. Only in the Church do we have our permanent city, an anticipation of the eternal tent we shall set up in the Kingdom of Heaven.

"Wherefore bear in mind that once you, the Gentiles in flesh," Paul tells the Ephesians, ". . . were at that time without Christ, excluded as aliens from the community of Israel, and strangers to the covenants of the promise, having no hope, and without God in the world. But now in Christ Jesus you, who were once afar off, have been brought near through the blood of Christ" (Eph. 2:11-13). "Therefore, you are now no longer strangers and foreigners, but you are citizens with the saints and members of God's household" (Eph. 2:11-14).

According to the New Testament, the Church is at one and the same time *ekklesía* and *paroikía*. "Let us therefore go forth to him outside the camp, bearing his reproach; for here we have no permanent city, but we seek for the city that is to come" (Heb. 13:13-14). The primitive Christian community, considering heaven to be its permanent homeland and not having any citizenship papers here on earth, thought of itself as a *paroikía*. Not only is each Christian a stranger and pilgrim, but the whole community as well (1 Pet. 2:11). Therefore the parish, in a biblical sense, is not the community of neighbors who live around the place of worship, much less any other territorial district, but rather a community of faith which lives as a stranger in this life, without the right of citizenship. "Therefore it seems to me," said H. Valesius in 1691, "that the Church on earth is only a foreigner or sojourner and that its home is in heaven."[4]

Toward the year 100 Clement of Rome wrote his first letter to the faithful in Corinth, beginning it: "The Church of God, which in Rome is foreign, salutes the

4 Cf. F.-X. Arnold, *ibid.*, p. 76.

Church of God which is foreign in Corinth." So too begins the letter of Polycarp: "To the Church of God, which is foreign in Philipos." Irenaeus, according to Eusebius,[5] called the Christian community a "paroikía." The same assertion appears in the synods of Antioch (268) and Sardis (342), and in the letter of Pope Julius I to the Church in Alexandria.[6] As a technical term, reserved exclusively to each local Christian community *hic et nunc*, the word "paroikía" was used from the middle of the second century on, as can be seen in the *Martyrium Polycarpi* (155) and in the writings of Dionysius of Corinth, Irenaeus, Apollonius, Eusebius, etc.

In the Old Testament the word "Qahal" meant the Jewish community, the people of God, Israel. In order to distinguish itself not only from the pagans, but from the Jewish community itself, the Christians did not translate "Qahal" as "synagogue" but rather "Church of God." Paul says: ". . . our citizenship is in heaven . . ." (Phil. 3:20). "For we know that if the earthly house in which we dwell be destroyed, we have a building from God, a house not made by human hands, eternal in the heavens" (2 Cor. 5:1). With regard to the pagans, the Christians consider themselves foreigners just like the Jews. With regard to the Jews, they maintain that their position has been established by Jesus Christ in order to make the pilgrimage toward the Father's house as a nation of the New Alliance. The situation of the Christian community is "parochial" in the etymological sense of the word. They live in a state of *diáspora*—of dispersion—among alien peoples and in foreign lands. Peter in his first letter, addresses himself to ". . . the sojourners of the Dispersion in Pontus, Galatia, Cappadocia, Asia and Bithynia, chosen unto the sanctification

5 Eusebius, *Hist. Eccles.*, V, 24, 14.
6 Cf. citations in F.-X. Arnold, *ibid.*, p. 76.

of the Spirit according to the foreknowledge of God the Father, unto obedience to Jesus Christ and the sprinkling of his blood" (1 Pet. 1:1).

The Christian communities that the Apostles founded after the coming of the Holy Spirit were called "Churches" although they actually correspond to our notion of a diocese and had a parochial flavor to them insofar as they considered themselves in a state of pilgrimage. This is not purely coincidental. The whole Church lived in each local community, injecting herself into a world not her own. Little by little, in the scientific language of theology, three distinct terms took shape: "Church," "diocese" and "parish." In the New Testament, nevertheless, these terms live together to indicate to us that their spiritual roots are the same.

From the moment when Jesus was recognized by His Apostles as the Messiah, the new messianic community visibly began to bud forth. On the other hand the leaders of Israel rejected Christ's mission. Hence, the Remnant of Israel took refuge in a new synagogue, formed by Jesus' disciples. The twelve Apostles have a special place there (Matt. 18:18), and above all, Peter (Matt. 16:19).[7] This New Alliance does not reject all the characteristics of the old one, but instead views itself as the one true heir of the Covenant which the patriarchs Abraham, Isaac, and Jacob made with Yahweh in another age. It claims for itself a new Spirit, which is the Spirit Jesus was to send from the Father after He fulfilled His promise to die, rise again, and ascend into heaven, the glory of God and the redemption of all mankind.

The Christian community, withdrawing from the

7 Cf. H. Kahlefeld, "Das Leben der Gemeinde nach dem Neuen Testament" in K. Rahner, *Die Pfarre* (Freiburg im Breisgau: 1956), pp. 41-43.

Jewish synagogue, recognized no other law than that of the Gospel, nor any leader other than Christ.

The first characteristic of the new Christian assembly is the fact that it is centered around the very person of the Lord, in order to share in His life.

Secondly, this Christian community is like a family, a family whose members are not united by bonds of blood but rather by the unity of those who do the will of God (John 4:31-35). In such a family it is necessary to forgive (Luke 17:3-4) and correct one's brother (Matt. 18:15-17) because the Father is merciful (Luke 15:1-32). Jesus is the elder brother who is never absent, because He told us that wherever two or three persons are gathered in His name, He will be there (Matt. 18:20). Everything that the sons ask the Father will be granted them (Matt. 18:19).

The third characteristic of the Christian community is its ability to take all kinds of men to its breast: rich and poor, cultured and ignorant, slaves and freemen, men and women, children and adults. Actually it is a community made up of the odds and ends of the world—the poor, the hungry, those who weep, etc., according to the spirituality of the Beatitudes (Luke 6:20-26). The figure of a child, which for the Jews was the personification of impotence and weakness, is also the image which Jesus used to illustrate the spirit that the members of His community should strive for: ". . . whoever does not accept the kingdom of God as a little child will not enter into it" (Mark 10:15), ". . . for of such is the kingdom of God" (Mark 10:14). "Whoever therefore humbles himself as this little child, he is the greatest in the kingdom of heaven" (Matt. 18:4).

Finally, anyone in that community who ". . . wishes to be first, he shall be last of all, and servant of all" (Mark 9:34). "For he who is the least among you, he is the greatest" (Luke 9:48). On earth the rulers of kingdoms like to "lord it over" their people (Mark 10:42) and there are those who "love the first places at suppers and the front seats in the synagogues, and greetings in the market place, and to be called by men 'Rabbi.' But do not you be called 'Rabbi'; for one is your Master and all you are brothers" (Matt. 23:6-8).

The birth and development of the Christian community was brought about through a calling from God and not by man's will. God called Abraham, Isaac, Jacob, and the Prophets. He may call at any time and in any situation, as in the case of the Apostles. In the New Testament, God's call is through Christ. "Come, follow me" (Mark 1:17), He told the Apostles whom He had selected (Mark 3:13). Christians are called, Paul tells us, ". . . in Christ" (1 Cor. 7:22; Col. 3:15). This is one of the many points of difference between Christ and the rabbis, since in the latter's communities the application for admission came from the disciples themselves.[8]

Jesus' disciples remain in His community as long as they follow Him. They must give up everything (Mark 10:28) and they will not be able henceforth to choose another master (Luke 9:61). Following Christ is the most radical decision a man can make in this world. "Go," Jesus tells the rich young man, "sell whatever thou hast, and give to the poor, and thou shalt have treasure in heaven; and come, follow me" (Mark 10:21). It is necessary to shed not only material possessions but earthly affections as well. "If anyone comes to me and does not hate his father and mother, and wife and children, and brothers and sisters, yes, and even his own life, he cannot be my disciple" (Luke 14:26). In the final analysis, to follow Christ is to imitate Him in His

8 K. H. Schelkle, *Jüngerschaft und Apostelamt* (Leipzig: 1958), pp. 17-18.

passion and His cross. "And he who does not carry his cross and follow me, cannot be my disciple" (Luke 14:27).

Another radical difference between Jesus' disciples and those who followed the rabbis is that the former never argue with their Master. Being a disciple of Christ is not a prelude to later becoming a master oneself, but rather a fulness of life itself.[9] The expression "to follow Jesus" is contained exclusively in the Gospels. The Acts of the Apostles speak of the "disciples of Jesus." Paul, deepening even more the relationship between Jesus and His disciples, no longer writes, "go with Christ," but rather, "live with Christ," or simply, "in Christ," since he speaks of the mystical Christ, the one we receive through faith and sacraments.

In short, we know that the first Christian community was a family of people chosen by God, weak by nature, whose head was Christ and where the greatest of all was a servant. They lived in Christ, with His Spirit, in the midst of a world where they felt themselves foreign because of their allegiance to the true homeland they longed to reach.

b) Ecclesial actions of the Christian community

1) *Preaching*

The day after Jesus cured in Capharnaum ". . . many who were afflicted with various diseases, and cast out devils" (Mark 1:34), His disciples said to Him: "They are all seeking Thee." He replied: "Let us go into the neighboring villages and towns, that there also I may preach. For this is why I have come" (Mark 1:37-38).

9 *Ibid.*, p. 25.

Proclaiming the message of salvation is Christ's first mission.

Without the word, the miracles would have no meaning (Mark 8:11). "The Spirit of the Lord is upon me because he has anointed me; to bring good news to the poor he has sent me, to proclaim to the captives release, and sight to the blind; to set at liberty the oppressed, to proclaim the acceptable year of the Lord and the day of recompense" (Luke 4:18-19). It was for proclaiming the Gospel and healing that the Apostles were sent, even more than for baptizing and teaching (Matt. 10:7). To the word they added the testimony of good works so that both might bring salvation. The Apostles had to select deacons when they began to realize that the demands of the growing Church required more attention than they were able to give, since ". . . it is not desirable," they reasoned, "that we should forsake the word of God and serve at tables. . . . But we will devote ourselves to prayer and to the ministry of the word" (Acts 6:2-4). Paul himself was to declare later on: "Christ did not send me to baptize but to preach the Gospel" (1 Cor. 1:17).

The spoken word has a tremendous force for the Oriental.[10] The whole of the Old Testament bears witness to the efficacy of the word of God. God spoke and things were made from nothingness (Gen. 1; Ps. 32:9; 106:20; Os. 6:5). "Is not my word like a fire, says the Lord, like a hammer shattering rocks?" (Jer. 23:29). "Your all-powerful word from heaven's royal throne bounded," says the Book of Wisdom 18:15, "a fierce warrior, into the doomed land." "For just as from the heavens the rain and snow come down and do not return there till they have watered the earth, making it fertile

10 Cf. H. Schlier, *Die Verkündigung im Gottesdienst der Kirche* (Cologne: 1953).

and fruitful, giving seed to him who sows and bread to him who eats, so shall my word be that goes forth from my mouth; it shall not return to me void, but shall do my will, achieving the end for which I sent it" (Is. 55: 10-11).

In the New Testament too, the word has the same creative force: "The words that I have spoken to you are spirit and life," said Jesus (John 6:64). The word of Christ is capable of curing corporeal (Matt. 8:8) and psychic ills (Mark 1:25) and even of raising the dead (John 11:43). The word of God is ". . . living and efficient and keener than any two-edged sword, and extending even to the division of soul and spirit, of joints also and of marrow, and a discerner of the thoughts and intentions of the heart" (Heb. 4:12; Thess. 2:13) it is stronger than any bonds (2 Tim. 2:9) and stronger than all the judgments of human foolishness (1 Cor. 1:12-23); it is capable of saving souls (Jas. 1:21) and sanctifying men (1 Tim. 4:5). This word is not primarily narration after the fashion of the Greek *logos* but rather a proclamation according to the concept of the biblical *logos;* it does not rest in the first place on truth but on salvation; it does not seek only the *verum* but also the *bonum;* it does not speak of men but to them; it is not concerned with the intellect but with the will, yet does not speak in general terms but in concrete ones. It is catechesis but not teaching; its nature is not static but dynamic; it is personal and historic with a soteriological, mystagogical, eschatological function.[11] It is not first of all a word bearing reconciliation, salvation, grace, life, etc., but rather it *is* reconciliation (2 Cor. 5:19), salvation (Acts 13:26), grace (Acts 14:3), life (Phil. 2:16), etc.[12]

11 C. Floristán, "El kerigma cristiano," *Lumen,* VI (1957), 291.
12 K. H. Schelkle, *op. cit.,* p. 64.

"Faith then," says Paul, "depends on hearing, and hearing on the word of Christ" (Rom. 10:17). The Apostle is a mediator of the word of God, a herald who proclaims the Good News. What matters is not the life of the messenger but rather the contents of the message itself, the *Kerygma.* In the New Testament, Christ is never called "Kerix," herald of God, since He is the proclamation itself. On the other hand, John the Baptist and the Apostles receive this title of "Kerix" and Paul in particular applies it to himself (2 Tim. 1:11). The translation of "Kerisein" as "preaching" is not altogether exact; it means much more. "Kerygma" is thus the cry of the herald and the publication of news. Christian kerygma is, in a broad sense, the contents of the proclamation of the Good News, of the general announcement of the word of God. And if we refer to the first news given to the non-Christians, we can say that the kerygma is the death and resurrection of Christ (1 Cor. 15:14).[13]

The kerygma, says Rétif, is the solemn, public proclamation of salvation through Christ, a proclamation made in the name of God (or by God Himself) to non-Christians, accompanied by signs and by power, which inspires faith, conversion, and a return to God in the souls of those disposed to receive it.[14] The word "kerygma" is found eighteen times in Paul, which points up the mission and the importance of Christ in the preaching to non-Christians. Christ is the very center of the proclamation, as can be seen in the preaching and the liturgical art of the first Christians.[15]

The first declaration of faith made by Peter (Acts

13 C. Floristán, *ibid.*, pp. 292-293.

14 A. Rétif, "Qu'est-ce que le keryme?" *Nouv. Rev. Théol.*, LXXXI (1949), 913.

15 J. A. Jungmann, "Das Kerigma in der Geschichte der kirchlichen Seelsorge," in *Katechetik* (Freiburg im Br.: 1953), p. 291.

2:14-38) is at the same time the first apostolic kerygma. In synthesis the first part of this declaration says (14-24): "Jesus of Nazareth, crucified and killed by unbelievers, was brought back to life by God." After the proclamation of the kerygma, that is to say its central content, Peter speaks of its prophetic fulfilment according to the Scriptures (25-36). Prophecy is the second fundamental element of the proclamation. And finally, as a consequence, a "metanoia" (change of heart) overwhelmed the listeners. "Brethren, what shall we do?" the listeners, pierced to the heart, asked Peter and the other Apostles. Peter replied: "Repent and be baptized every one of you in the name of Jesus Christ for the forgiveness of your sins; and you shall receive the gift of the Holy Spirit" (37-38).

Kerygma therefore constitutes the central fact of the proclamation of the word of God. Notice how Peter proclaimed a salvific fact in a prophetic context and how he consequently achieved a moral regeneration. A similar analysis could be made with the other kerygmas contained in the Acts of the Apostles, as for example that of Peter to the multitude after the curing of the beggar (3:12-26), the conversion of the pagan Cornelius (10:34-43) and Paul's appearance before Agrippa and Bernice (26:2-33).[16]

"The word of God," declares Schelkle, "is in a hurry to fulfil itself, to engender life, to found a community of listeners. For this very reason, where there is the word of God, there is always the Church. The word created the Church—it created the beginnings of the Church through the division of society into believers and nonbelievers."[17] Just as the sacrament acts where

16 Cf. Rétif, *op. cit.*, p. 920; a complete list of nineteen kerygmas contained in the Acts of the Apostles.

17 K. H. Schelkle, *op. cit.*, p. 71.

it is received with faith, so too the word acts when it is heard with faith. Christ is the object of the faith, but He himself creates this faith through His word.

The word of God begets Christian community and it is truly proclaimed and heard only where the Church exists. There are many forms of preaching but they are not authentic unless they correspond to tradition. For this reason, only those witnesses who have received the tradition can indicate what the word of God is and send messengers to announce it. In the local Christian community, born thanks to the strength of the word of God, only those who serve the community in a biblical sense can announce the word so that the community may grow as a Church.

The most operative form of proclamation is the sacramental form. According to the New Testament, word and sacrament form a single unit: "For as often as you shall eat this bread and drink the cup, you shall proclaim the death of the Lord, until he comes" (1 Cor. 11:26). "The sacrament is coördinated with the proclamation in such a fashion that it can be considered a kind of proclamation, whereas the word has a sacramental character."[18] The foundations and roots, not only of the proclamation but of the liturgy as well, are found, according to Paul, in the proclamation of the Lord's death, sacramentally carried out as a commemoration by the Christian community.[19]

Several times the New Testament speaks of a service or ministry of the word, a *diakonia tu logou.* The Apostles were the servants of the word, since the word had been given them earlier. However, so that the word might be

18 *Ibid.*, p. 77.

19 H. Schlier, *op. cit.*, p. 68. Cf. C. Floristán, "La palabra y el sacramento en la acción pastoral," *Scriptorium Victoriense,* VIII (1961), 288-327.

preserved in them incorrupt, Jesus sent them forth "two by two" (Mark 6:7). The community must make sure of the purity of the word. Paul unmasked some types of preaching not practiced according to tradition. "Some indeed preach Christ even out of envy and contentiousness, but some also out of good will" (Phil. 1:15). Nevertheless, the deciding factor is not the preacher's ethical conduct but rather the word itself, in view of the fact that it is the word of God. ". . . in every way, whether in pretense or in truth, Christ is being proclaimed; in this I rejoice, yes and I shall rejoice" (Phil. 1:18). Naturally, the preacher ought to ". . . walk uprightly, according to the truth of the gospel" (Gal. 2:14); he should speak "not as pleasing men, but God" (1 Thess. 2:4), "renounce those practices which shame conceals, avoid unscrupulous conduct" (2 Cor. 4:2), without "adulterating the word of God" (2 Cor. 2:17). There are also some ". . . who do not serve Christ our Lord but their own belly, and by smooth words and flattery deceive the hearts of the simple" (Rom. 16:18).

The responsibility for proclaiming the word of God does not rest exclusively with those officially sent, but rather belongs in a certain way to all the members of the community: "When you come together each of you has a hymn, has an instruction, has a revelation, has a tongue, has an interpretation. Let all things be done unto edification" (1 Cor. 14:26). After the Apostles were taken before the Sanhedrin, as we read in the Acts, and after Peter had spoken and prayed, ". . . they were all filled with the Holy Spirit, and spoke the word of God with boldness" (Acts 4:31).

The Church is Church of the Word for many reasons, Schelkle maintains.[20] The most profound reason is the fact that Christ is the Word made flesh. Each local

20 K. H. Schelkle, *op. cit.*, p. 83 ff.

Church ought therefore to be, not just at the outset, but in its continuous formation as well, a Church of the Word.

2) *Worship*

"There is no doubt," says H. Schlier, "that according to the New Testament the community forms itself essentially in worship."[21] Worship is essential to any religious community.

Naturally, the Jewish community also had its liturgy, but judging by what our Lord says in the Gospels, this liturgy reached the point where its primitive spirit had been corrupted. Jesus recalls the words of Yahweh: "I desire mercy and not sacrifice" (Matt. 12:7), and He restored the meaning of the Lord's Day, since "the Sabbath was made for man, and not man for the Sabbath" (Mark 2:27). He made it clear that real purity is not in outward rites or in foods, but rather in the intentions of the heart (Mark 7:14-23). Thus He said: ". . . if thou art offering thy gift at the altar, and there rememberest that thy brother has anything against thee, leave thy gift before the altar, and go first to be reconciled to thy brother, and then come and offer thy gift" (Matt. 5:23, 24). Jesus respected the Jewish religious feasts and even the priestly and devotional authority, but He always sought the inward spiritual significance. The temple is worth more than the gold, since it sanctifies it, just as the altar is higher than the offering (Matt. 23:16-22). For this reason he drove the money-changers from the temple (John 2:14-16).

Jesus not only restored the real meaning of the Jewish liturgy, but by His death He instituted the New Alliance's form of worship. "Destroy this temple," He

21 H. Schlier, *op. cit.*, p. 17.

told the Jews at the time He threw out the greedy dealers, "and in three days I will raise it up." "He was speaking of the temple of his body," comments John (John 2:19, 21). The legacy of worship which the Lord left us is none other than the proclamation of His death; thus the celebration of the Eucharist constitutes the heart of the liturgy. *Unde et memores . . . offerimus.* For Paul, preaching is the proclamation of Christ crucified and the solemn celebration of the commemoration of this event is the proclamation of Christ's death. Therefore, the Gospel is united to the Eucharist, and the word to the sacrament.[22] The goal of the proclamation of Christ's death or its representation in the celebration of the Lord's Supper is the Communion in which we are given the Body and Blood of Christ as spiritual food (1 Cor. 10:16, 17). The Christian community will continue to carry out this action ". . . until he comes" (1 Cor. 11:26). All preaching of the word and every act of worship must be based on the proclamation of this unique event which constitutes the cornerstone and very axis of salvation history. Man is justified or condemned depending on the spirit with which he participates in the celebration of Christ's death.

Originally, the preaching of Christ and the Apostles was accompanied by the miraculous curing of the sick. The word was always accompanied by a deed. The word of salvation was attended by equally salvific works, since healing the effects of sin found in sickness and death is conquering sin itself. "For I do not make bold to mention anything but what Christ has wrought through me to bring about the obedience of the Gentiles, *by word and deed,* with mighty signs and wonders, by the power of the Holy Spirit" (Rom. 15:18).

But the great act with which Christ accompanied the

22 *Ibid.*, pp. 25-27.

Kerygma or Good News which he brought to a sinful world from His Father, is the celebration of the Last Supper, ". . . on the night in which he was betrayed" (1 Cor. 11:23), shortly before His death on the Cross. There it was that the Church was born and there it is that the foundations of any ecclesial community are laid. The Church, we have said, is a Church of the Word; true, but it is something more—it is a Church born from the side of Christ and which grows, in the eucharistic celebration, with the proclamation of the Lord's death. This death broke the bonds of death through the resurrection and fulfills the complete meaning of the word of God in the Scriptures with the Parousia of the *Kyrios*. Eschatological time wherein all sense of ecclesial community is born and constructed, in virtue of the Word and the Eucharist, unfolds from Christ's death "until he comes."

The celebration of the Eucharist, although the Christian community's central act of worship, is not its only act. The New Testament refers to other great salvific actions carried out by Jesus' disciples through the sacraments.

The first of all these actions, which were later to be called sacramental, is that of Baptism. Christ ordered this to be performed upon those who, in virtue of the proclaimed word, already believed (Matt. 28:19; John 4:2). "For you were buried with him in Baptism," Paul said to the Colossians, "and in him also rose again through faith in the working of God who raised him from the dead" (Col. 2:12). By erasing their sins, Baptism solemnly introduces catechumens into the ecclesial community. Thus, the Christian unites himself through Baptism with the Lord's death and resurrection (Cf. Rom. 6:1-11).

Another sacramental sign clearly expressed in the

New Testament is the imposition of hands. Through prayer and the laying on of hands, the baptized received the Holy Spirit (Acts 8:17-19; Heb. 6:2) and the Apostles communicated the power which they possessed as ministers sent by God (Acts 6:6; 13:3).[23] In short, all the sacraments, insofar as they are sensible signs of sacred actions which sanctify man, are found more or less explicitly expressed in the New Testament, at least as regards their fundamental substance.

A third form of worship manifested in the New Testament, along with the eucharistic celebration and the sacraments, is that which the assembly of the baptized carried out in the spirit of Paul's exhortation: ". . . in psalms and hymns and spiritual songs, singing and making melody in your hearts to the Lord, giving thanks always for all things in the name of our Lord Jesus Christ to God the Father," ". . . subject to one another in the fear of Christ" (Eph. 5:19-21; Col. 3:16). It is for this reason that the hymns of Mary (Luke 1:46-55), of Zachary (Luke 1:68-79) and Simeon (Luke 2:29-32) were composed. Other formulas such as confession (Phil. 2:5-11), hymns to Christ (1 Pet. 1:18-21; 2:21-25; 3:18-22), etc., were also employed. Actually, the Christian community made the most of its time (Eph. 5:15) and filled itself with the Holy Spirit in a liturgical prayer which at the same time is a form of proclamation of the word of God (Col. 3:16). It preceded or was frequently linked to the thanksgiving or Eucharist. In this way the liturgical prayer which the New Testament indicates and which later was to constitute the Church's *laus perennis,* in so far as it is an act of worship and officially ecclesial, is a sacred action indispensable to the perfect building up of the Christian community.

23 K. H. Schelkle, *op. cit.,* pp. 95-97.

3) *Pastoral care*

The Kingdom of God, around which Jesus' preaching is built, is a present and future reality. It is of the present in that it reaches men through Jesus Christ. It is of the future since it will reach its plenitude with the Lord's Parousia, when ". . . God may be all in all" (1 Cor. 15:28).[24] However, Christ did not bring a doctrine about the Kingdom of God, but instead brought that very Kingdom in His person, through preaching and miracles, Kerygma and His death.

Christ Himself *is* the Kingdom of God. For this reason, entrance into the Kingdom is gained only through faith in Christ. With the Apostles, the Kingdom of God is inseparable from the name of Jesus Christ (Acts 8:12; 28:32). The Kingdom of God is distinct from all human kingdoms and opposed to Satan's, whose forces have battled those of the Savior since the first appearance of sin in the world and which will continue until the end of time.

The Apostles were the Kingdom's first collaborators. Not only did they proclaim the Gospel and the Lord's death but they were also the guardians of the flock won with Christ's truth and blood.

"Obey your superiors and be subject to them, for they keep watch as having to render an account of your souls" (Heb. 13:17). The shepherds of the Christian flock must, like the Good Shepherd, be slaves to their sheep. The Apostles call themselves slaves (*doulos*) and servants (*diákonos*). This relationship of service was apparent in the Evangelists as well as Paul, and is inconceivable as a purely human affiliation. The idea of service deeply characterized the disciple: "Whoever wishes to become great shall be your servant; and who-

24 Th. Filthaut, *Das Reich Gottes in der katechetischen Unterweisung* (Freiburg im Br.: 1958), pp. 10-11.

ever wishes to be first among you shall be the slave of all; for the Son of Man also has not come to be served but to serve, and to give his life as a ransom for many" (Mark 10:43-45). "Both the Acts of the Apostles (20:24; 21:19) and Paul (Rom. 11:13; 1 Cor. 3:5; 2 Cor. 6:3) call all the missionary and apostolic work of an Apostle a function of service."[25] Even preaching and worship are the ". . . ministry of the word" (Luke 1:2; Acts 6:4) and ". . . service . . ." of the liturgy (2 Cor. 9:12).

The Christian community was subject to Christ through the service of the Apostles and disciples. "Not that we lord it over your faith," Paul told the people of Corinth, "but rather we are fellow-workers in your joy; for in faith you stand" (2 Cor. 1:24). The word "diakonía," unknown in classic Greek writings, appears in the New Testament to indicate ministry or function. Exercising a ministry in the Church is so radically different from possessing a function in the world, that the New Testament even uses a new word meaning "service."

Christ is the Good Shepherd, who gives His life for His sheep (John 10:15) and knows them even as His father knows Him. There were pastors in the primitive community, along with the Apostles and prophets, whose function was also charismatic. "Tend the flock of God which is among you, governing not under constraint, but willingly, according to God; nor yet for the sake of base gain, but eagerly; nor yet as lording it over your charges, but becoming from the heart a pattern to the flock" (1 Pet. 5:2-3). The spiritual shepherds are, in the final analysis, the fathers of the community. Paul thought of Timothy, Onesimus, Titus and all believers as sons, just as Peter felt toward Mark. "For although you have ten thousand tutors in Christ, yet you have not many fathers.

25 K. H. Schelkle, *op. cit.*, p. 37.

For in Christ Jesus, through the gospel, did I beget you" (1 Cor. 4:15).

"The apostolic writings of the New Testament," writes Schelkle, "declare that the apostle ought to be the *norm* and *form* of his community and all the Church."[26] Paul considers himself as an example to be imitated (2 Thess. 3:7; 1 Thess. 1:6; 1 Cor. 4:16; 11:1), in the sense that the Lord lived in him. Thus, Christ is the Christian's norm inasmuch as He appears in the apostle. "When one understands the New Testament with exactitude he sees that an apostle of the Church and a shepherd of the community are not only masters and guardians but saints as well, that is to say, a saint in the New Testament sense of the word, not an example of virtue so much as a clear example of God's choice and grace."[27]

And finally, the New Testament also points out a norm of conduct to the apostle and the disciple. It is above all their poverty which stands out. Jesus ". . . instructed them to take nothing for their journey, but a staff only—no wallet, no bread, no money in their girdle; but to wear sandals and not to put on two tunics" (Mark 6:8-9). God's grace sufficed; they had to be detached from all temporal ties. Paul was even to make his living with his hands. "Gladly therefore I will glory in my infirmities," he declared, "that the strength of Christ may dwell in me" (2 Cor. 12:9).

The Apostles, without material means, nevertheless had the power to "cure the sick, raise the dead, cleanse lepers, and cast out devils" (Matt. 10:8). Their joy lay in the Kingdom of God, which had already begun and would reach its fulness at the end of time. "Now if the ministration of death, which was engraved in letters upon stones, was inaugurated in such glory that the

26 *Ibid.*, p. 45.
27 *Ibid.*, p. 47.

children of Israel could not look steadfastly upon the face of Moses on account of the transient glory that shone upon it, shall not the ministration of the spirit be still more glorious? For if there is glory in the ministration that condemned, much more does the ministration that justifies abound in glory" (2 Cor. 3:7-9).

All the characteristics of the first Christian community as recounted in Scripture, beginning with the biblical concept of *Paroikía,* can be applied to the Christian parish community. The primitive community continues to be the norm for all the rest which have been established down through time and space since the days when the Apostles first began their mission of proclaiming, by word and deed, the death and resurrection of our Savior.

CHAPTER TWO

THE PARISH IN HISTORY

1. Origins

The parish came into being in a strictly pastoral sense much earlier than as a strictly canonical concept. It can be said that the parochial institution, outwardly regarded as an ecclesiastical organization, was born towards the end of the third or start of the fourth century. But long before, with the start of the local churches, the internal and pastoral structure of the parish was under formation.

We have mentioned in the preceding chapter the characteristics of the primitive community; now let us examine those of the local churches, since the parishes were born within them and in accordance with their apostolic spirit.[1]

At the outset the direction of the Church was in the

1 Cf. an excellent résumé of the history of the parish in A. A. Blochlinger, *Die heutige Pfarrei als Gemeinschaft* (Zurich: 1962), pp. 33-150.

hands of the Apostles, who had received from Christ the command to preach the faith, baptize believers, and serve the baptized (Matt. 28:19ff). Just as the Apostles devoted themselves to missionary activities such as founding new communities, the prophets and teachers contributed with their charisms to the subsequent development of the faithful (1 Cor. 12:28ff; Acts 13:1; Eph. 4:11; Did. 11:13-15). These teachers and prophets did not share in the ministry of administration, but their influence was notable. The number of the Apostles' successors likewise grew with the imposition of hands.

On the other hand, bishops, priests, and deacons sprang up in the Christian communities situated in pagan lands, through prayer and the imposition of hands (Acts 20:17-28; Phil. 1:1; 1 Tim. 3:2-12; 5:17, 19; Tit. 1:5, 7; Did. 15:1; 1 Clem. 42:44), with a ministry of their own which was of an organizing nature. The Acts of the Apostles makes specific mention of the bishops ". . . placed to rule the Church of God" (20:28). About the year 96, Clement of Rome declared in his letter to the Corinthians that the Apostles had appointed bishops and deacons to the ministry, with the charge that they in turn choose trustworthy men to continue their ecclesial functions (*Let. to Cor.* 42:4; 44:2). In a word, the members of the Church are divided into two groups: those with a ministry, and the faithful. Together, they form the universal Church (Ignatius, *Smyrn.* 8:2).[2]

Those who directed the Church appear in the Bible, for the most part, with the name of *elders* (priests) or *overseers* (bishops), which names were used indiscriminately. Collectively, they constituted a college, called the *presbyterium* (presbyterate) (1 Tim. 4:14), similar to

2 K. Bihlmeyer and H. Tüchle, *Kirchengeschichte* (Paderborn: 1952; 13th ed.), I, 102-104. Cf. L. Duchesne, *Origines du culte chrétien* (Paris: 1909, 4th ed.).

the Jewish council of elders which directed synagogues in areas of the diaspora. The college was presided over by an *episcopos* or bishop, who little by little was differentiated from a plain presbyter up to the point of possessing the powers of a present-day bishop. It is apparently not clear how all this came about; mention of it appears for the first time in the letters of Ignatius of Antioch written about the year 110. So it is that the episcopate has continued from the time of the Apostles.

In the primitive Church we find two kinds of Christian communities. The first is made up of the Churches founded by Paul in the big cities but which sometimes had communities in the surrounding regions (2 Cor. 1:1; Acts 19:10). However, although presided over by "presbyters" or bishops (Phil. 1:1; Acts 20:17, 28; 14:23), these small communities were headless since, in the final analysis, it was the Apostle who gave them unity. Not until the hour of Paul's martyrdom was approaching were these Churches to be governed by his successors, like Timothy in Ephesus and Titus in Crete, with the same Pauline powers.[3] Gradually these direct successors of the Apostles began taking up residence in the cities of their regions, forming the priestly college they presided over.

A second type of local church is found in the Apocalypse (1:20; 2, 3) with a purely monarchical and sedentary form of organization, called *Johannine* by J. Colson.[4] This Church was reduced to the actual limits of a city and presided over by a bishop, who summed up in his person the powers of apostolic succession and was surrounded by a college of priests and deacons.

3 J. Colson, "Qu'est-ce qu'un diocèse?" *Nouv. Rev. Théol.*, LXXV (1953), 472. Cf. Colson's other works on the primitive apostolic ministry.

4 *Ibid.*

These two ecclesiastical systems were rapidly fused to create the local church, presided over by the bishop of a city where, from his *cathedra* he oversaw, in faith and charity, all the territory covered by the minor churches governed by ministers of lesser rank. From the second century on, the bishop was teacher, liturgist, and pastor of the local church, with the presbyters forming his council or senate. Until the end of the third century only the bishop celebrated the Eucharist, surrounded by his concelebrant priests, as we read in Hippolytus (*Apostol. Trad.*, 24). Nevertheless, it does seem that there were cases in the days of Ignatius when the Eucharist was celebrated by the bishop's delegates because of the long distance between the episcopal see and certain small communities (cf. *Smyrn.* 8).

With time these local churches, which were frequently called *paroikías* and presided over by a bishop, were divided into small communities under the charge of one or more priests. The unity of the whole local church and the entire ministry continued in the hands of resident bishops. We know from Pliny the Younger's well-known letter that Christianity spread through rural areas at the start of the second century. As the number of Christians grew, it became impossible for all of them to go to the city on the Sabbath to celebrate eucharistically the memory of the Lord with the bishop. In the big cities the problem was similar because the assembly rooms were inadequate to accommodate the increasing numbers; the great basilicas, we must remember, had still not been built. In Rome for instance, some private houses served as places of worship and residences of the priests and minor clergy. This was the origin of titular churches, at first with the name of the owner of the house and later under the protection of a famous martyr or saint. Toward the year 300 there were fifteen or twenty such titular churches in Rome. Pope Fabian (236-250) divided Rome into seven districts in memory of the first seven deacons. Rural churches also began to appear from the third century on. We know that there were priests and teachers in Egypt (*Eus.* VII, 24:6), a *diaconus regens plebem* in Spain (Council of Elvira, c. 77) and *corepiscopos* or rural bishops in Syria (*Eus.* VII, 30:10). Their head continued to be the bishop in the city.[5]

In this fashion small communities corresponding to our present-day parishes began springing up in the countryside and city. The limits of the local churches corresponded to those of the Roman provinces, and from the fourth century on, the bishops were called *metropolitans*. Division of the Church into provinces took place in the East during the third century but not until somewhat later in the West.

All those who received the Word of God with faith were baptized. During the second century catechumens were subjected to a test period which lasted from two to three years, with Baptism being administered twice a year: at Easter and Pentecost. Normally the bishop conferred it; only in case of necessity did priests, deacons, or laymen baptize.

The Eucharist, as a community meal and a memorial of the death of Jesus Christ, was celebrated at sunset after the agape. Because of many difficulties the celebration was transferred at the end of the Apostolic era (beginning of the second century) to the early morning hours and united to the liturgy of the word. A particle of the Eucharist (*fermentum*) was carried by the acolytes from the place of episcopal worship to the titular churches at the precise moment that the officiating priest gave the *Pax Domini*. This was done as a real symbol of communion or unity in Christ with the bishop.

5 K. Bihlmeyer and H. Tüchle, *op. cit.*, p. 111.

Until the fourth century penance was a sacrament presided over by the bishop, and the sinner publicly confessed his sins before the clergy and community. Even matrimony was carried out with the express approval of the bishop.

In short, the parish gradually became more and more delineated during this first period in the Church. The normal unit of the Church was the diocese, which Irenaeus in the second century called *paroikía*, but soon the titular churches were to spring up as small Christian communities—forerunners of the parish communities. The pastoral accent in this first stage fell more on faith and the word than on the sacraments.[6] This does not mean to say that the center of all Christian life did not lie in the celebration of the Pasch and the death of the Lord but rather that each local church, existing as a *paroikía* or wayfarer in a pagan world, accentuated the *service of the word* as a prime requisite for the beginning of the salvific process brought about by the death, resurrection, and ascension of our Lord Jesus Christ.

2. After the Peace of Constantine

In the years following the Edict of Constantine, the Church's situation changed. In a certain accidental sense Christians no longer lived in a foreign land, in *diaspora*. Little by little they began to lose the eschatological meaning that the local *paroikía*-church had for the first Christians and instead, the juridical idea began to gain ground. By the year 410, Christians could already say in the words of the recently composed Te Deum, "Throughout the world the holy Church acknowledges Thee."

With the Peace of Constantine the great persecutions

6 F.-X. Arnold, *Dienst am Glauben* (Freiburg im Br.: 1948), p. 18.

decreed by the Emperors from Decius to Diocletian came to an end. During this first great missionary period clergy and laity alike lived from the same well-springs: the word of God, the Scriptures and the divine actions in worship. Christian literature caused pagan literature to recede, the theological concept of dogma molded in the great Councils was matured by the ensuing ideological struggles, and an endless number of martyrs and saints were invoked as heavenly intercessors. Justly could Tertullian write to the pagans: "Crucify us, torture us, condemn us, crush us. . . . We become more numerous whenever our number is lessened by you; the blood of Christians is seed" (*Apol.* 50).

The fourth and fifth centuries were the classical age of the great Fathers, from Athanasius to Cyril and from Hilary to Jerome, not forgetting the most extraordinary of them all: Augustine.[7] While the patristic age lasted, Christianity displayed an eminently missionary character owing to the heedfulness of the great bishops to the proclamation of the word of God and the maintenance of centers of catechumens. Constantine's conversion gave the Church new status and strength, at least in its outward organization. It is equally true that a subsequent decline followed with the death in the seventh century of the last Father, Isidore of Seville. Dissolution of the catechumenates ensued, which in turn caused a devitalization of pastoral activity in that field of Church action which through the proclaiming of Kerygma, constitutes not only the beginning of the salvific process but also the inseparable sustenance of the eucharistic meal. Since that time forward, a shadowy half-light has obscured the patristic thinking which held that in a certain

7 Cf. Van der Meer, *Augustinus der Seelsorger* (Cologne: 1955, 2nd ed.).

sense the Christian continues to be a catechumen all his life.

Around the fourth century the word "paroecia" meant a local or particular church, as is confirmed in the second edition of Eusebius of Caesarea's *Ecclesiastical History* (c. 324 or 325). Obviously, from the second half of the fourth century on, the word "parochia" meant diocese. It is found with this acceptation in the writings of Paulinus of Nola, Jerome and Augustine.[8] For quite some time *parochia* and diocese meant the same thing, to the point that in the sixth century the two were still used indiscriminately.[9]

The first rural churches with a permanent organization were established in Gaul around the beginning of the fourth century. This evolution was held up by the Arian heresy until Constantine's death in 361, but later on it would acquire new vigor, receiving a strong impulse in the sixth century. In these churches, worship was already celebrated, but only the bishop's church had a baptistery. As the number of faithful grew, the bishops granted their rural priests certain privileges. These churches even came to form a *presbyterium,* with deacons, subdeacons, lectors and porters, similar to the bishop's. Although the naming of the rectors of these churches was up to the bishops, little by little through the influence of the nobility, these appointments began to be made without the bishops' consent.[10]

From the third century there were Christian communities in the country governed by *corepiscopos.* The danger that each of them might come to consider himself as an authentic *episcopus,* successor of the Apostles,

8 Fliche-Martin, *Histoire de l'Eglise,* (1939), IV, 578-579.

9 Cf. H. E. Feine, "Kirchliche Rechtsgeschichte," in *Die Katholische Kirche,* vol. 1 (Weimar: 1954, 2nd ed.).

10 W. M. Plöchl, *Geschichte des Kirchenrechtes,* 3 vols. (Vienna-Munich: 1953-59).

prompted the Councils of Ancyra (314) and Antioch (341) to forbid their naming priests and deacons without the consent of the bishop of the city. At the Council of Sardis (343) towns and small cities were prohibited from having bishops, so that the dignity and authority of the latter would not be decreased. As a result of these rulings, the "rural bishops" or *corepiscopos* passed to secondary rank and finally disappeared in the eighth century. After that time the ministry in the smaller towns was in the hands of ordinary priests, with a worship independent of the episcopal worship, although subject to the bishop's supervision. Solely in the big cities was the custom observed of having only one solitary celebration of the Eucharist at which consecration was performed by the bishop, even though there were several churches.

Starting in about the fifth and sixth centuries many rural churches, called "parochiae," with a priest of their own, were formed in France and Spain. So it was that the parish system began its rapid spread, especially among the Germanic peoples whose civilization was typically rural. At the same time that this decentralization grew for the sake of pastoral reasons, the bishop's authority necessarily developed proportionately. Formation and delineation of diocesan and parochial rights were due above all to the synods. The bishop's duty was to visit the parishes and celebrate synods, whereas the rectors or pastors could preach and baptize, visit the sick, bury the dead, and give private penance, although not public reconciliation. Beginning about the fifth century there were papal decrees setting up parish limits. Among the Germanic peoples (Catholics as well as Arians) there began to sprout up *ecclesiae propiae,* constructed by the lords at their own expense and on their own extensive domains. The duty of paying tithes was already in existence among the Carolingians. For this reason the number of private churches began growing from the seventh century on, especially in France—built for the purpose of obtaining benefices. In pastoral circles the idea of the *beneficium* was acquiring importance to the detriment of the apostolic idea of *servitium*. From pastoral circles this idea gradually crept into canonical statutes.

Within the parochial field there sprang up, along with the *ecclesia baptismalis,* such additional places of worship as the *oratoria, basilicae, capellae, tituli minores,* etc., in part to facilitate the attendance of the faithful at acts of worship and in part as signs of devotion to certain saints.

These "private churches" enjoyed parochial rights from the eighth century on. Some monasteries and convents, anxious for the *beneficium,* tried to incorporate parishes, setting off an intense fight between parochial and conventual groups. The Church had become a powerful landowner in all the territory converted to Christianity, so that each diocese possessed not only the mother church or cathedral, but also more or less vast possessions in all the area where the bishop had jurisdiction. Although the city where the bishop had his see might frequently have several churches, nevertheless it constituted but one parish.

During the seventh century the rural clergy already had their parishes organized, without the obligation of celebrating the big feasts with their respective bishops. During the sixth century there were some parishes headed by archpriests. Seventh century bishops and councils protested against the foundation of such churches, which were handled like private property, but actually there was nothing they could do to halt this lay usurpation of power. Parochial and episcopal organisms as well as monastic ones grew considerably richer during this period, thanks to the numerous private offerings "for the help of souls."

Offerings of bread and wine in accordance with liturgical standards were already common in the sixth century; later on, offerings of cash were introduced, to be divided among the church, the poor, the clergy, and the bishop. Still later, the alms would be divided among the clergy, the bishops, and the poor.

3. The Middle Ages

This period of Church history brought new political, ecclesiastical, and cultural concepts. The geographical orbit where religious events were taking place shifted from the Mediterranean to Central Europe. The evangelization of the Germanic peoples continued, reaching a peak of intensity between the eighth and eleventh centuries. Civil authority encroached upon the ecclesiastical sphere and the Church carried out political and social functions. Meanwhile, the Eastern Church, while not influenced by the Middle Ages, nevertheless suffered from the inroads of Islam, was torn by internal strife, and experienced such tension in its relations with the Latin Church that it finally broke with Rome in 1054.

The properties held by ecclesiastical groups, which ultimately amounted to a third of state territory, eventually constituted a strong temptation to the imperial powers. Charles Martel (714-741) brought about the first large-scale secularization of Church property. He was followed in this move by his two sons around 743-745, later on by Charlemagne, and frequently by the nobility throughout the ninth and tenth centuries.

In nations with a long tradition of Christian faith, like France, Italy, and Spain, there was a close-knit network of rural parishes in the tenth and eleventh centuries. They extended rapidly toward central and northern Europe during the tenth century as a result of evangelization.[11] Established in the *vici,* these parishes were clearly called *parochiae.* The *villa* frequently corresponded to the limits of a parish, although there were also parishes which took in several *villae.* Conversely, there were *villae* with several parishes. The parish clergy were directed by a *presbyter,* also called rector. Since the *cura animarum* was his responsibility, he also came to be called *curatus.* The parish links between the presbyter and his flock were very close, although almost exclusively canonical. He performed his duties under the juridical and economic watchfulness of the bishop, who provoked frequent disputes with his pastors because of his demands regarding certain donations. The relationship was thus similar to that existing between the lords and their vassals. Like the cathedral, the parish church had a patrimony (*beneficium*) comprising the church, the cemetery, the property and goods fund, oblations, chapels, and, above all, tithes. Tithes were obligatory during the Carolingian era and collecting them was the parishes' task. At first the tithes pertained only to agricultural products, but starting in the ninth century the councils did everything possible to extend them to all other fields.

Once Gregory VII (1073-1085) undertook his reform with the famous protest against investiture, the moral level of the clergy took an upswing in all the Christian kingdoms, especially from the start of the twelfth century on. The monks' powerful influence in episcopal circles became particularly notable in the eleventh and twelfth centuries, when even vacant sees were filled from the ranks of monks. But the investiture evil came from the cathedral chapters, due to secular influence. Start-

11 *Ibid.,* (1940), VII, 265 ff.

ing with the twelfth century, lay influence over parish churches declined, as can be seen from the two Lateran Councils (1127 and 1139).[12] Although the process was not without its difficulties, the feudal system was gradually transformed in the sense that the laity lost influence over ecclesiastical riches and once again respected the priests' prerogatives. The parishes won back from lay power were appropriated by the religious orders, so that by the end of the twelfth century all the religious orders had parishes. This favored reform in a sense, above all with regard to the parochial clergy and the people, but there was always the risk that the religious orders might themselves succumb to worldly influence, as did indeed happen. Lay investiture was followed by nicolaism and simony.

Innocent III (1198-1216) undertook another great religious reformation. The thirteenth-century clergy, although infected by many vices, including greed for riches, followed their spiritual mission at least in part. There was no lack of bishops who acted effectively, but actually the renovation of the *cura animarum* came about mainly through the mendicant orders, particularly the Franciscans and Dominicans. With their vows of stability broken, the new monks went to the cities. In 1281, Martin V gave them a bull which, with the permission of their superiors, enabled them to preach and hear confessions anywhere. This hurt both the feelings and the economy of the parish clergy. In the year 1300, Boniface VIII issued a decree providing that the mendicants could not preach in public squares without permission of the bishop, nor inside the churches without the permission of the respective pastors. Other difficulties were created by the matter of confession and the right to bury in consecrated ground. The dispute lasted

12 *Ibid.*, IX, 144.

almost up to the Council of Trent—for three centuries.

Medieval religious unity was already resting on a powder keg long before Luther came into the picture, as can be seen from the schism of Avignon. Similarly, there was a general feeling of discontent within the Church. Gradually, instead of wishing expressly for a reform "of the head and members" as had previously been true, the cry became: "Return to the Apostolic Church."[13] From the start of the fourteenth century to the end of the fifteenth, long before Luther, outcries were heard against the curialism and clericalism of Rome. The roots of these evils can be traced to the practice of giving benefices, as was fully conceded by the Avignon popes. Finally, Lortz declares, "from the fourteenth century on, there was a growing *theological insecurity* in the ecclesiastical sphere,"[14] especially in England and Central Europe. If such an insecurity existed among theologians, it was naturally much more profound among the insufficiently trained lower clergy.

During the fifteenth century private altars and Masses were multiplied, producing a rupture in the parochial community. Individual conscience was awakening to the detriment of the community conscience and humanism, the great movement of the time, placed man at the center of all considerations. From Alexander VI through Julius II to Leo X, the tide of humanism rose as high as the papal throne. Leo X's official entrance into Rome as pope resembled a sacramental procession, with the place of honor occupied not by the Blessed Sacrament but rather by the pope himself. One Good Friday, Erasmus heard a humanistic lecture given in the pope's chapel wherein not a single word was said either about

13 J. Lortz, *Wie kam es zur Reformation?* (Einsiedeln: 1950), p. 29.

14 *Ibid.*, p. 34.

Christ or His Passion.[15] Curialism reached an extraordinary level; the administration of the Church was marked by arbitrariness and a multiplicity of ecclesiastical favors, almost simoniacal acts, and above all a growth in material riches.

Under such circumstances the Roman Curia could scarcely understand the protests and desires of the new reformers. When Albert of Brandenburg was named Bishop of Mainz at the age of twenty-five, after already being named titular bishop of another diocese, he paid twenty-five thousand gold ducats to Rome through the Fuggers to acquire still a third bishopric, according to the Catholic historian Lortz. *Cura animarum,* preaching, and the sacraments were given far less attention by the papal curia than ecclesiastical business affairs. The situation among the cardinals and bishops was no better. The lower clergy, practically cut off from the higher clergy, was almost exclusively made up of peasants. In fact the Church had become the property of the clergy and the priestly ministry was a flourishing business.

The fifteenth century was one of contradictions. There were often the outward signs of religion without its true spirit. Popular acts of piety were abundant, but lacked the sincerity of real liturgical prayer. The Mass, which among other things is a bond of unity, was considered a private devotion and the sacraments were not infrequently thought of as almost magical; Confirmation was seldom and badly conferred. The saints, on the other hand, occupied a predominant place in the Church and their relics produced marvelous effects. At such a time of natural faith, the study of the sacraments and their *ex opere operato* effectiveness held the first place in theology. It is true that there was preaching and an abundance of it, but its content was a long way from the

15 *Ibid.*, p. 65.

primitive Kerygma. There was no absence of religious mysticism or personal prayer, although there was an excess of subjective emphasis, perhaps due to nominalistic influences. An exemplar of the period is Thomas à Kempis' *Imitation of Christ,* a book which had a special influence on the *devotio moderna.* Despite everything, it was a time of serious religious thought, as one can also see from the art of the period.

Here then is the picture about 1500: "A Catholic world with an extremely rich ecclesiastical life, an abundance of clergy and numerous convents and monasteries. The Church, and no one else, was the unquestionable ruler of all sectors of life, private as well as public. And yet an inconceivable catastrophe suddenly took place. What had gone wrong? Things had been changing radically for some time but had gone unnoticed. Life was Catholic judging by appearances, but in reality this picture was false."[16]

In brief, a profound rebellion was being forged from the thirteenth century on. Theological insecurity, religious indifference, and a deep feeling of discontent with the clergy were to explode as the Protestant Reformation. In the meantime, parish priests and religious orders went on arguing about who would collect the parish profits.

4. The Reformation

The ecclesiastical revolution set off by Luther in 1517 was without precedent in history. It opened the door to religious individualism as a protest against subjection to an objective dogmatic authority, a life of sacramental worship, and an ecclesiastical hierarchy.

16 *Ibid.*, p. 75.

The priority given to *sola fides* smashed the theological and pastoral unity of the Church. For all practical purposes it sapped her life's blood of the salvific value of the liturgy, reducing its essence to the word of God—the sole Lutheran sacrament. The Protestant Reformation did not achieve what it set out after and instead of reforming the whole Church merely divided her. The Counter-Reformation did not succeed in its aim of uniting the divided Church either, but it did enable Rome to clean its own house, thanks to Trent.

The Church's first reaction to the Protestant attempt at reform was positive, as can be appreciated pastorally from the 1566 catechism of St. Pius V. Later on, theological polemics were extended to the pastoral field with the result that St. Peter Canisius' and Cardinal Bellarmine's catechisms (toward 1600) already had an anti-Protestant flavor. At the same time, Protestant concepts had strongly anti-Catholic shadings.

The Council of Trent was an extraordinary event for the *cura animarum* in general and the parish in particular. Its effects on them were as great as those which its definitions and canons had upon dogma. The council gathered together and unified the reforming tendencies of many previous synods. Without the existence of these synods and the people who directed them, the council would never have been able to make the great advance it brought about. The main thoughts of Trent in regard to pastoral activity were as follows:

1. The bishop is pastor of his diocese, which must once more become the heart of the *cura animarum*. There is no effective substitute for the bishop and for this very reason he has the duty of residence. He himself ought to preach to the people in his diocese and take care that all the parochial communities hear the word of God.

To this end he should visit them frequently. He must pay special attention to the training of his clergy and establish seminaries for this purpose.

2. The pastor is second in line of responsibility for pastoral activity, for whom the same things said about the bishop hold true: the duty of residence, the obligation to preach, the prohibition against obtaining prebends, and most concretely the care of the religious education of youth.

3. In order for the pastor to be able to fulfill all these duties, the parish ought to have very precise limits within a reasonable territory. When the pastor is unable to handle all the parish activity by himself, he should have assistants. If parish churches do not exist, they should be constructed.

4. Relations between the parochial clergy and the religious clergy ought to be excellent. The apostolate of the latter is not denied, but instead it is suggested that it serve as an aid in the needs of the diocese, especially in the preparation of the diocesan clergy.[17]

The pastoral reformation was carried out by groups of religious, especially Jesuits. They spread parish missions, built retreat houses and gave religious instruction to the young in their schools. In all truth there were few bishops capable of carrying out the Trent reforms, with notable exceptions like St. Charles Borromeo.

Through a historical consequence which invariably results from a lack of both community spirit and liturgical devotion, the remarkably individualistic post-Trent parishes were void of a deep sense of liturgical worship, although popular pious practices abounded. Perhaps out of fear of falling into Protestant attitudes, the impor-

17 W. Croce, "Die Geschichte der Pfarre" in *Die Pfarre* (Freiburg im Br.: 1956), pp. 25-26; cf. A. Schrott, "Pfarre und Pfarreseelsorge im Wandel der Zeiten" in *Die Pfarre* (Vienna: 1953), p. 12.

tance of faith in justification was scarcely treated at all, even though Trent had firmly declared: "Faith is the foundation and root of all justification." The idea of the Word as bearer of grace, and indeed salvation, was set aside or reduced in Aristotelian fashion to being simply a bearer of knowledge or, at most, of truth.

If one compares sixteenth- and seventeenth-century catechisms with that of Trent, an impoverishment of the kerygmatic spirit appears. More than the *veritas quae creditur*, it was the *fides qua creditur* that was stressed. The value of religious decision, man's personal obedience to the preached word of God, and faith as a salvific path and motive of sacramental life were all admitted but insufficiently emphasized.[18]

We see then that, starting with the Council of Trent, the parish took on a new pastoral clarity; upon it and the diocese rested the entire religious reform undertaken by the Council fathers. The parish unquestionably took on a juridical aspect which was needed, on the other hand, to clarify a confused state of affairs. Ever since then the word "parish" has meant a clearly defined territory forming part of a diocese; this concept was later to pass intact into the Code of Canon Law. The idea of the benefice did not completely disappear but the ultimate desire that the Council instilled in pastors was that of serving the "salvation of souls." Parochial pastoral work, however, suffered the consequences of anti-Protestant polemics; the more frequent and bitter they became, the more void of real content. The pastoral accent fell on the sacraments more than the Word, although the people never came really to participate in the liturgy. Despite everything, the people grew in their piety and many saints of the period have been canonized. Toward the end of the seventeenth century, devotion to the Sacred Heart

18 F.-X. Arnold, *Dienst am Glauben*, p. 28.

of Jesus began in France; in Italy the month of May was dedicated to Mary. These devotions were extended to the universal Church in 1765 and 1815, respectively, and found a fertile field in the parishes.

5. The Enlightenment and the Nineteenth Century

Once the Peace of Westphalia (1648) had put an end to the religious struggles, Catholic-Protestant polemics also gradually cooled off. Perhaps through a lack of great theologians and personalities, the reform of Trent was not continued as the thinking of the Council fathers had envisioned. The modern states which began appearing had such great strength that they were easily able to intervene in ecclesiastical affairs. The period was characterized by the Enlightenment (*Aufklärung*) which originated in Germany and rose out of the Renaissance separation of faith and reason, and of religion and culture. As a consequence of this new movement, people began drifting away from revealed doctrine and the Church, with a subsequent secularization of law, science, economy, morality, and, in a certain sense, all culture. The world was faced with the turbulent period of ideas which was to come to a head in 1789 with the French Revolution.

Not only did secularization affect the cultural domains which in earlier times had been the exclusive patrimony of the Church, but all too often the interest of churchmen themselves centered more on cultural than on religious matters. While it is true that there were eighteenth century attempts at reform of ecclesiastical discipline, pastoral theology, and even the parish itself, the basis of such attempts lay in ideological movements of the period. The state's absolute sovereignty over the Church was recognized and the reformers of the day saw the pastor as a teacher of the people who would promote their welfare.[19] Parish boundaries were determined by state decree. During this century many monastic riches passed into the hands of the state or became parish possessions. It is undoubtedly true that at the time there was a number of monasteries all out of proportion to the small number of parishes, but the states' decisions were hardly motivated by pastoral reasons; they were instead prompted by the period of weakness the Church was going through.

In the eighteenth century, the catechism entered a new stage, and the testing of one new catechism after another has gone on ceaselessly ever since. Accent was on religious education, which was state sponsored by that time, but there was no attempt to go into the contents of catechesis and preaching in any depth. What was of interest was the endeavor made in language, in logical order, in summarized exposition and clarity—in a word, in method. The liturgy was considered a servant of education, which in turn had a strong moralistic bent. It was not the mystery of Christ's redemption that was stressed but rather its importance in maintaining the human virtues. Christ's presence in the Eucharist attracted much more attention than the Mass as a sacrifice and sacrament. In general, a rationalistic morality dominated faith. The Church appears in the thinking of the theologians of the period almost exclusively in her visible and hierarchical aspect. In the ministry, primacy was given to the juridical function rather than to the inner spirit, and the Christian apostolate became clericalized.

A pastoral movement of great importance sprang up about this time in Germany, a product of the Catholic faculty at Tübingen, but this effort never managed to

19 A. Schrott, *op. cit.*, p. 13.

gain the upper hand. Sailer (1751-1832) renewed biblical studies; he was influenced by Romanticism, which he attempted to apply to the Church, in a search for a fervent and living Christianity. He attacked rationalistic, moralistic, and utilitarian pastoral thought; grounded in Scripture and supported with history, he went straight to the essence. Later on, Hirscher (1788-1865) undertook a kerygmatic reform. He was convinced that preaching is the principal task of Christianity and attacked the scholasticism of his time, accusing it of deforming the Gospel. He published a catechism along the lines of the one published at Trent.

Nevertheless, toward the middle of the nineteenth century the works of Perrone, Kleutgen, and Franzelin contributed to the triumph of neo-scholasticism. These works were rigorously theological but with a tendency toward being more systematic than historical and biblical. Scholasticism was implicitly identified with the Gospels and the catechisms of the period are nothing more than a résumé of scholastic theology with no history of salvation, the Bible, or liturgy. The Jesuit missionary Deharbe (1800-1871) composed a catechism of an anthropocentric nature which followed this neo-scholastic line. It was eventually translated into fifteen languages and came to exercise a great influence in the religious education of youth. Besides its anthropocentric character, it had an anti-Protestant bias to it and a moralizing tendency also.

These nineteenth-century writings had a very definite influence on the development of religious life. Priestly theological preparation took on a neo-scholastic look, as did popular religious training at the parish level.

The position of the parish in the nineteenth century was characterized on one hand by the absolutist influence of the state and on the other by sociological changes under way as the result of the technological evolution of that time. Never in all the history of the Church was the parish pastoral problem more critical than at the end of this century. The big cities and newly created industrial centers attracted great masses of workers who were completely out of contact with the Church. "It is often forgotten," says R. Mols, "that the Church had not *lost* the working class, but rather that this class had been formed completely outside of the Church as a consequence of three great transformations which dominated nineteenth century social history: the population explosion, industrialization, and urban concentration, and also because the Church did not effectively assume her responsibility in this triple transformation that was under way."[20]

Because of state control, the growth rate in the number of parishes was no greater in the nineteenth century than in the eighteenth despite the fact (thanks to technical and medical progress) that the population grew at an incalculable rate. Thus it was that excessively large parishes grew up in the big cities; in some cases they were larger than some Italian dioceses. The problem is still with us today in European cities and difficult to solve now because the proper remedies were not applied in time.

Parochial piety acquired a typically individualistic note in the second half of the nineteenth century and start of the twentieth century, with an absence of parish community spirit. Sunday had been celebrated for several centuries not as the day of Christ's resurrection —as the Lord's Day—but as a day of rest and of sacred duties for the benefit of one's soul. Preaching dealt more with the duty of going to Mass than with the eucha-

20 R. Mols, "Croissance et limites de la sociologie religieuse," *Nouv. Rev. Théol.*, LXXVII (1955), 152.

ristic celebration itself and more was said about the obligation of resting on Sunday than that of sanctifying holydays in spirit and in truth. The sacraments, which came after the commandments in the catechism, were simply means of living a moral life. Sunday prayer had become diluted into a thousand prayers marked by a sense of spiritual negotiation. The Bible was an unknown, dangerous, and unintelligible book. The liturgical year was supplanted by a calendar year full of triduums, novenas, and septenary observances, while distinctions between the social classes were strictly maintained in the administration of the sacraments. Christianity, instead of being celebrated, was administered. The primitive Kerygma had disappeared from preaching and it was the idea of the benefice rather than service that attracted people to the ministry. Morality replaced dogma in preaching, canon law took the place of pastoral theology in the *cura animarum,* and metaphysical speculation edged salvation history and the Bible out of dogma, while passive routine supplanted active participation in the celebration of the mysteries of the Lord.

The parish, meanwhile, was forgotten in most cases and played scarcely any role at all in the events and the currents of ideas of the time. There were indeed conscientious pastors, as there have always been throughout the history of the Church, but the overall mass of parish clergy and their pastoral work were going through a period dangerously lacking in vitality. This is what the great Cardinal Gomá of Barcelona had to say about the pastoral scene in 1918:

> The people do not sing; St. Paul's *commonentes vosmetipsos* is no longer the law in liturgical assemblies. Preaching, a social function, has been displaced from the social liturgical acts. What is more, it has become personal and private insofar

as it does not originate in the needs and demands of the liturgy but instead in the occasionally fanciful personal criterion of the preacher. Each church is a club-house for a variety of confraternities, each with its own inclosure or altar, its own group of faithful, its saint and its feast day, its own set of pious practices. As in the Church of Corinth, there are sometimes antagonisms in the sacred unity of the temple. Within one city there are divers temples and shrines, each with its own particular worship and customs. While they steadily step up their enticements and organize showy services with lights and music, eloquence and flowers, but *without liturgy,* the mother church of the area—cathedral or parish church—remains empty, with only the ministers themselves to celebrate the liturgy, *the social service of our Holy Church.*[21]

6. The Twentieth Century

The Church undoubtedly needed to centralize and concentrate, a task undertaken in the second half of the nineteenth century. On the one hand she began to reawaken to her spirituality and on the other hand to shed her temporal and political power. The Vatican Council (1869-1870) represented an awareness and acceptance of responsibility of extraordinary proportions, especially for speculative theology and law. Starting with Leo XIII the popes began to make pastoral judgments on the great events of their times with a determination and clarity which recalls the greatest pontiffs of history. In particular, St. Pius X carried out a pastoral reform such as perhaps no single pope since the Council of Trent had done. He promoted the codification of canon law

21 Cardinal Gomá, *El valor educativo de la Liturgia* (Barcelona: 1918); cf. citation in *Tu parroquia y tu pastor* (Madrid: 1944), p. 40. For the pastoral study of the *Aufklärung,* see the writings of Arnold.

and reorganized the Roman Curia; he provided norms for religious instruction, diocesan seminaries, and theological studies; he urged early and frequent communion, and, to top off this impressive list of achievements, he promulgated a new breviary and issued regulations for the reform of sacred music. It can well be said that Pius X is the great pope of the modern pastoral movement which has had and is having so many repercussions on the parochial ministry.

Benedict XV continued the reforms of Pius X and during his pontificate the Code of Canon Law was published (1917) in which there is a wise compilation of canons on parochial law, as we shall see later on. In 1922 Pius XI created Catholic Action as the movement of lay participation in the Church's hierarchical apostolate; the movement has had a great reverberation in parish life. Following this trend, Pius XII, in all his talks, displayed an enormous affection and concern for the parish, greater than any other twentieth-century pope before him. All his great decisions, especially priestly and liturgical ones, have had tremendous consequences for parish vitality, particularly with reference to the pastoral life which a parish should have—its constant nourishment by the word of God as well as by the celebration of the sacramental mysteries.

With the new job of pastoral renewal undertaken by Pope John XXIII through Vatican Council II, the parish will without a doubt receive a tremendous new influence. It is to be hoped that the Constitution on the Liturgy will exercise a very great influence on the parish community, but it would not be sufficient for the parish to renew itself liturgically if at the same time it did not undergo an apostolic and missionary renewal.

It can truthfully be said that the parish is today an exciting topic of interest, not only in connection with the pastoral renovation presently being carried out by the Church's ordinary apostolate, but also in relation to the preoccupation of contemporary theologians with the subject. Since for all practical purposes the life of the Church is concentrated in each of her parish-community units, it is therefore true that a renewal of the reality and idea of the parish means a renewal of the whole Church. We know that the parish was born historically and did not come into being by divine right. We also know that this history has never been interrupted since the third or fourth century, the time of its birth. Today we can freely discuss and dispute many of its aspects, but judging from history, one thing is beyond doubt: in essence the parish constitutes the cornerstone in the pastoral life of Christ's Mystical Body.

CHAPTER THREE

THE PARISH IN THEOLOGY

1. The Church—Mystical Body of Christ

The greatest occurrence of recent years to play a profound role of renewal in the thinking of theologians and in Christian pastoral life has probably been the rediscovery of the Church as the Mystical Body of Christ.

The ground was ready and fertile thanks to the studies of modern theologians, deeply inspired by the ecclesiological concepts of Newman and Möhler; the definitive light was cast in 1943 by Pius XII's encyclical *Mystici Corporis Christi*. It can be said that ecclesiology today occupies a fundamental place within the ecclesiastical sciences. R. Grosche goes so far as to say that "the religious problem today consists in the essence and reality of the Church."[1]

This rediscovery has been extremely important for pastoral work, since current theological-pastoral thought

1 R. Grosche, "Pilgernde Kirche" (Freiburg im Br., 1938), p. 23.

revolves around the Church as the Kingdom of God established in history. "The Church," writes Arnold, "as a multiple and inexhaustible object of theological attention essentially and necessarily presents three aspects. To our eyes, the Church appears as something which has developed historically, as an invariable reality which has survived down through time, and as a responsibility to be continued through the years to come. These three aspects have to be studied by theology: the first historically and biblically, the second systematically, and the third through practical theology."[2]

All the efforts of a number of modern theologians to work out carefully a theology of the parish have had their starting point in the theology of the Church. Their separate conclusions have been different but their points of departure have been almost identical.

What is the Church? Faced with such an inexhaustible reality, the answers to this question have naturally been highly varied. Yves Congar declares that until a few years ago and with few exceptions, Catholic theology "has treated the Church as an objectively existent institution—which is naturally true—but very seldom as an assembly of the faithful and a living community representative of its action; that is to say, it has considered her in her immutable essence and very little as existent in time."[3] The *De Ecclesia* manuals have reflected the external hierarchical and sociological aspect of the Church with only a few notes regarding her mystery. The study of her structure has outshone consideration of her life.[4] We can be said to be witnessing in our time

2 F.-X. Arnold, "Grundsätzliches und Geschichtliches zur Theologie der Seelsorge" (Freiburg im Br., 1949), p. 6.

3 Y. M.-J. Congar, *Vrai et fausse réforme dans l'Eglise* (Paris, 1950), p. 9.

4 St. Jaki, *Les tendances nouvelles de l'Ecclesiologie* (Rome, 1957), p. 12.

a remarkable ecclesiological renewal, since there is a transition from an apologetic treatment to a dogmatic one, from a study of structure to a study of life, from reflection on juridical questions to consideration of mystical ones.

a) Definitions of the Church

There are different views possible with regard to the Church, just as there are with Christ, says Journet. We can look at Jesus as: a) a man, b) an exceptional man, and c) the Word made flesh. Analogously, the Church can be viewed as: a) a religious society, b) an extraordinarily valuable religious society, and c) the Mystical Body of Christ.[5] Similarly, Congar distinguishes the following three planes: a) *Ecclesia* in so far as it is an aggregate of hierarchical personalities, b) *Ecclesia ex hominibus* in so far as it is an assembly of the faithful or the Christian people, and c) *Ecclesia, id est fides et fidei sacramenta* in so far as it is a divine institution.[6]

In the final analysis there are two ways to consider the Church, depending on whether we define her according to her created or her uncreated causes. With regard to her uncreated causes (Christ, Spirit, God), "the Church is the Body of Christ, the Bride of Christ, Christ's flock, the Gospel continued, the dwelling place of the Holy Spirit and the Blessed Trinity—the house, the tabernacle, the city, people, and kingdom of God."[7] And with regard to her created causes, the Church is the Communion of Saints. Christ is the beginning and the guiding principle of the Church. In Christ the individual, the divine nature joins itself to His own nature through the personal and hypostatic union, but as the total Christ,

5 C. Journet, *Théologie de l'Eglise* (Bruges, 1958), chap. I.
6 Y. M.-J. Congar, *op. cit.*, p. 98.
7 C. Journet, *op. cit.*, p. 18; Bossuet, Lt. 28.

the divine nature is joined to the collective human nature by the union of grace and inhabitation.

Thus in Scripture we encounter definitions of the Church, for example: "the dwelling of God with men" (Apoc. 21:3); "a holy nation . . . the people of God" (1 Pet. 2:9-10). The best definition, according to Pius XII's encyclical, is the one inspired in Paul's Epistle to the Colossians (1:24): The Church as the Body of Christ. Bossuet's definition is also famous: "The Church is Jesus Christ spread abroad and bestowed among men, Jesus Christ whole and entire, Jesus Christ perfect man, Jesus Christ in His fullness."[8]

One of the first statements which can be based on these same references is that the Church is eternal and historical, a divine gift and a mission to be accomplished: "at one and the same time terrestrial and celestial, temporal and eternal, present and eschatological, human and divine, active and contemplative, collective and individual, personal and suprapersonal, united in love and ruled by laws, visible and invisible."[9] Its nature therefore is theandric; to reject one of its two aspects is to destroy it. The Church, permanent incarnation of the Savior, perpetuates His mystery.[10] Exaggerated mysticism is as dangerous as naturalism. "In order to safeguard life," Cardinal Suhard writes, "the modernist sacrificed forms; in order to safeguard forms, integralism sacrifices life."[11]

1) *The continuing incarnation of Jesus Christ*

Thus, the Church is the continuing incarnation of Jesus Christ in the world. Instead of quantitative in-

8 Cf. mention in Journet, *op. cit.*, p. 400.
9 St. Jaki, *op. cit.*, p. 263.
10 Card. Suhard, *Growth or Decline?* (Notre Dame, 1960), p. 41.
11 *Ibid.*, p. 65.

crease, there is an organic unfolding. The Church is at once, as Suhard puts it, an *être* (being) and a *devenir* (becoming); changeless *être* in its invisible reality, and *devenir*, century after century, in its visible reality.[12] The world has need of the Church for its life and the Church needs the world for its growth and perfection. Herein lies the Church's pastoral task: the communication of Christian life, the incarnation of the total Christ. Consequently the Church is the sole mediatrix. Cyprian was right when he said: "there is no salvation outside the Church" (*Ep.* 73:21) and "no one can have God for his father who does not have the Church for his mother" (*De cath. eccles.* 6; *Ep.* 74:7).

2) *The communion of saints*

In the second place, the Church is a community of the redeemed. The very word "Church," even when applied to one church in particular, immediately brings to mind the idea of an assembly of people.[13] "The Church's path," says Peterson, "leads from the earthly to the heavenly Jerusalem, from the city of the Jews to the city of the angels and saints. The fact that it exists between the earthly and the heavenly *Polis* constitutes its essence. For this reason the Church's character consists in the fact that Christians have abandoned the earthly Jerusalem to seek a future city, whose builder is God (Heb. 11:8-10), since on earth they have no permanent city (Heb. 13:14), just as Abraham had none."[14]

12 *Ibid.*, p. 42.

13 L. Cerfaux, "La théologie de l'Eglise suivant saint Paul," (2nd ed. Paris, 1948), p. 300.

14 E. Peterson, *Das Buch von den Engeln* (Leipzig, 1935), p. 13.

b) The ministry of the Church

The ministry of the Church can be reduced to two great acts: the preaching of the faith and the celebration of the sacraments of the faith within the ecclesial system.[15] Its final end, as Congar has said, consists in causing all the substance of the first Adam to pass bit by bit into the second; that is to say, it comes down to progressively summarizing all things in Christ.[16] To accomplish this mission, the Church passes through a series of historical stages, more or less intermingled.

1) *An evangelical community*

There is an exact correspondence between the Church (which means "the convened") and the Word of God. There is a real Church only where the true Word is present and vice versa. We have seen that according to the New Testament the Word creates the Church and only the Church proclaims the true Word. "The Church is properly so called because it calls to itself and gathers together," says St. Isidore.[17] The Church thus constitutes a *congregatio hominum* when it is a *divina convocatio.*

This calling is rightfully exercised only by those who have received the mission of building the Church. But the only means of transmitting the Gospel, the Good News, consists in having received it through *tradition.* Therefore, only the envoy of the Church is able to convoke; that is, the person authorized by the bishop, since the Church is in the bishop.

The Church, as an evangelical community or a community of people called together by the Word, is basically

15 "Apostoli et eorum sucessores sunt vicarii quantum ad regimen Ecclesiae institutae per fidem et fidei sacramenta" (III, q. 64, 2 ad 3).

16 Congar, *op. cit.*, pp. 170-171.

17 Cf. mention in H. Fries, *Die Kirche als Anwalt der Mensch der Gegenwart* (Stuttgart, 1954), p. 137.

founded on the fact that Jesus Christ is the Word of God. Arnold says: "The Word of God has a triple meaning. On the first level the Word is inner-Trinitarian dialogue by which the essence of the Father is formulated in the Son. The Father is the ultimate root of the Word."[18] "On the second level," Arnold writes farther on, "the Word of God becomes dialogue between God and man. This is already so at the time of creation. . . . The culminating point of this dialogue is the incarnation of the Logos in the fullness of time." The third level is preaching, as we shall see later on.

If the Church is the continuous incarnation of the Word of God, with Christ the Word of the Father, the Church will also be the uninterrupted proclamation of the Gospel. So it is that the Church in its roots is an evangelical community.

2) *A sacramental community*

Although the word is the *beginning* of salvation, it is not all; the word necessarily leads to the sacraments.

We say that the Church is a *communio sanctorum.* Since the genitive *sanctorum* comes from *sancta* and not *sancti,* the Church is a community gathered around holy things. It is first of all a community brought into being through the word, but in the final analysis it is an evangelical community centering around acts of worship. Naturally it is also a communion of saints embracing all men who have responded with faith to the proclaimed word and who participate in the supreme proclamation of Christ's death, whether in a state of pilgrimage (Church Militant), purification (Church Suffering), or glorification (Church Triumphant).

18 F.-X. Arnold, "La predicación como proclamación de la palabra de Dios," in *Comunidad cristiana parroquial* (Madrid, 1959), p. 233.

The Church is a sacramental community because it is definitively the original sacrament; it is the sacrament of Jesus Christ just as Jesus in His humanity is the sacrament of God, understanding sacrament to mean "a symbol of grace and the visible sign of invisible grace."[19] "The Church contains divine reality in such a real and objective fashion that when one is in contact with the visible Church one feels this divine reality contained within her," maintains Semmelroth.[20] The Church is the sacrament of humanity, as each of the sacraments is each man's. Moreover, the sacraments bestow invisible grace only in contact with the Church, the original sacrament. Christ is the image of all sacramentality since He is the visible form of the invisible God; that is, Christ's humanity is the Epiphany of the Word of God. "There is no other sacrament of God except Christ," says St. Augustine.[21]

The Church sprang forth, like all the sacraments, from the side of Christ. "Belief in the passion gives efficacy to the sacraments."[22] It came forth from his side just like the blood and water did—the symbols of Baptism and the Eucharist (cf. John 19:34). Together with the spirit, which is truth, the water and blood are the three great witnesses (1 John 5:5-8). The baptism of Christ is the beginning, and the blood of His passion the final fullness; in between is the spirit of truth contained in the Good News. These three witnesses are the three great salvific actions of the Church: the truth, Baptism, and the Holy Eucharist.

Just as creation, accomplished through a word, preceded the Incarnation which culminated in the blood of

19 D. 876.
20 O. Semmelroth, *Die Kirche als Ursakrament* (2nd ed. Frankfurt, 1955), p. 43.
21 *Ep.* 187, n.34; *PL* 38, 845.
22 *Sent.* IV, d. 1, a.4, sol.3 ad 3; III, q.62, a.5 ad 2.

Christ, so too the Church as an evangelical community preceded the Church as a sacramental community. God first spoke and revealed Himself; His people with Christ as the head of Humanity, replied with the sacraments: a descending prophetic movement complemented by an ascending one of worship. The Church—word of God—is ceaseless incarnation; as the eucharistic sacrifice of Christ, she is a continuous ascent to the Father in the Holy Spirit. This intercommunication involves movement from God to the world through the word, and from the world to God through Baptism and the Eucharist. Without an evangelical community there is no baptismal community and without a baptismal community there is no eucharistic community. "Because the bread is one, we though many, are one body, all of us who partake of the one bread" (1 Cor. 10:17). It is the Eucharist that brings the Church into action just as it is the Church that brings the Eucharist into action.[23] Wherever the Eucharist is celebrated the Church is more intensely present, "since not only is Christ present in this celebration, as Savior of the Body and as salvation and Lord of the Church," states Karl Rahner, "but furthermore the unity of the faithful with Christ and among themselves is brought about in a more visible and intimate manner in the eucharistic banquet."[24]

2. The Diocese, the Total Church

a) Eternal and historical

The Church, by continuing the Incarnation of Christ on earth, is necessarily linked to time and space. It is

23 H. de Lubac, *Meditation sur l'Eglise*, 3rd ed., 1954, p. 113; cf. B. Schultze, "Eucharistie und Kirche in der russischen Theologie der Gegenwart," *Zeitschr. f. Kathol. Theol.*, 77 (1955), 257-300.

24 K. Rahner, "Zur Theologie der Pfarre," *Die Pfarre* (Freiburg im Br., 1956), p. 32.

for all time and for now; it is for all space and for here; it is eternal and it is historical. To try to reduce it to pure community is to tear it apart; to subject it too much to time and space, like just another society, although admittedly a perfect one, is to root out its very life. Until the Parousia, the Church will have to live with the constantly growing tension between the eternal and the historical communities. But in reality it is only one community: the *communio sanctorum,* the Mystical Body of Christ. The Church is pure in so far as it is a communion gathered around holy things (*sanctorum* from *sancta*); it is impure in so far as it comprises the communion of saints (*sanctorum* from *sancti*). Without men there is no Church, just as Jesus Christ cannot exist without human nature. For this reason the Church has a twofold personality: it is a mystery of God on earth and it also has the form of a human community. The Church came before the *congregatio fidelium,* that is it precedes its members and begets them. Congar states: "The Church in the first sense of the word (an institution of salvation), ceaselessly performs works of salvation for the Church in the second sense of the word (the people of God and a community of the faithful)."[25] The Church is not of the world but lives in the world. Necessarily, through the ministry and sacraments of the faith, it should provide the men of some determined time and place with truth and life, so bountifully present in Christ. It follows the expansion and history of mankind, applying to it the Redemption. "The Lord himself will give his benefits; our land shall yield its increase" (Ps. 84:13).

b) Universal and local

This perfect community of all those who are loyal

25 Congar, *op. cit.,* p. 112.

to Jesus Christ as their Savior, and to the Father through Him, lives locally. In the same way that the consecrated bread is one but in many particles, so too the Church is one in all its many communities. "Many in one, and the whole, mysteriously, in each," wrote St. Peter Damien.[26]

In the first chapter we saw that the first ecclesial communities were founded by the Apostles. In the Pauline as well as the Johannine communities the unity was provided by an Apostle whose vocation directed him, through a mandate from Christ, to evangelize all peoples. The community of Christians under the direction of an Apostle was called a "Church" in the New Testament. Without the intervention of the Apostles or their direct successors no Churches were founded; there was no such thing as a private Church. The Church that is not apostolic is not an authentic Church. For this reason it is not possible to admit of a Christian community or a single Christian that is not or has not been subject to a bishop, a successor of those Apostles. Not only is a private Church without a bishop inadmissible, but a universal Church without a bishop is unthinkable.

When an Apostle or one of his successors could no longer be physically present for all the functions of an ecclesial community, other and different offices began to appear in the ministry, such as the *presbiteroi* and the *episcopoi,* with the mission of "explaining the Scriptures, watching over the group's development, assuring the laying on of hands in the future, and celebrating the Eucharist."[27] The Apostle was present in all these gatherings, not physically or sacramentally like Christ, but instead through his function and above all through

26 Cf. mention in Lubac, *op. cit.,* p. 127.

27 O. Rousseau, "Communauté ecclésial et communauté monastique," *La Maison-Dieu,* LI (1957), p. 11.

his word. When all the Apostles had died, their communities were to go on hearing their voice through the words written in their letters.

"Diocese," according to the etymology of the word, is the assembly of the people of God gathered together around the Lord Jesus, represented by a bishop.[28] Whether composed of a single city (the Johannine type) or a city and region (Pauline), a diocese is essentially a local church or group of headless communities which constitute a church through reference to a bishop. Colson says that the diocese is "the vocation of a city or a region and its population to fulfill, in its own place and era, the Body of Jesus Christ; the people of God around a visible center—the bishop—successor of the Apostles. For Ignatius of Antioch the community of each local church represented in fact, at the start of the second century, the vocation to unity of all the Christian people. Putting his expression into our words as best we can, it is the *people in God.*"

The radical difference between the universal Church and any other society consists in the fact that all of the universal Church is found within the local church. Actually, this is a pre-Christian Jewish concept, since all the people of God are present in each of its communities and, of course, in the holy Remnant of Israel. The Church is not divided as one divides a country into provinces; the universal Church is composed, true enough, of local or single churches but this occurs through concentration. According to K. Rahner, "the universal Church, considered as a reality in the deepest sense of the word, is necessarily a local church; all the universal Church is

28 J. Colson, "Qu'est-ce qu'un diocèse?" *Nouv. Rev. Théol.*, LXXV (1953), p. 471; cf. *ibid.*, *L'évêque dans les communautés primitives* (Paris, 1951).

visible in the individual one."[29] This happens precisely because (as we saw earlier) the Church is, in the first place, the continuous incarnation of the Word of God in the world, and in the second place, a hierarchical society of a juridical sort. Because of the character of incarnation of the Son of God which it carries out historically, the Church is seen in its fullness in the proclamation of the Lord's death, when it celebrates the Eucharist. But the Eucharist can only be celebrated locally. The universal Church is thus integrally present in the local one. "The Eucharist, as a local event, not only happens exclusively *in* the Church, but indeed the Church itself becomes the entire event, in the most profound sense of the word, in the local celebration of the Eucharist."[30] Thus we once again identify the Eucharist with the Church, as some Orthodox theologians have done.

Consequently, the local church is necessarily of divine origin, since it is an authentic church, a local concentration of the universal Church.

c) Marks of the local church

1) *The bishop*

The bishop makes it possible for Christ to be found wherever two or three are gathered together in His name. "Because the Apostle has committed the task of vigilance to his care, the bishop is the center. Just as Christ is the bond of union for all the members of the Church, the bishop is the bond of union for his flock. Among everyone, he is the visible element of a holy unity. The clergy and the faithful ought to be in agreement

29 K. Rahner, "Primat und Episkopat, Eine Überlegungen über Verfassungsprinzipien der Kirche," *Stimmen der Zeit* CLXI (1957/58), p. 328.
30 *Ibid.*, p. 330.

with him and in communion with him, just as the Apostolic Churches ought to be, on the other hand, in communion with one another."[31] To the Apostolic Fathers, the bishop was an image of the Father, a representative of Christ. The priesthood which has come down from Christ through the Apostles as an apostolic gift is bound only to the bishop, not to the *presbyterium*. The bishop alone possesses the *cathedra*. "It would seem," says Luykx, "that the presbyterium's only function has been that of somehow bringing about the most direct fruit of the incarnation of Christ in the local church through the bishop."[32] A close relationship of a nuptial sort united the priesthood of the presbyters to that of the bishop. The *presbyterium* of a particular church, with the collaboration of the nearest bishops, used to name a new successor when the bishop of their diocese died. When the *presbyterium* disappeared, the bishops of a province became the ones who named, before the people, the legitimate pastor of that local church. During the period following a bishop's death when his see remained vacant, that church was referred to as a "widow" by the liturgy.

The close union of the priests and faithful with their bishop prompted Ignatius of Antioch to tell them: "You are united to the bishop like the strings to a lyre. By this perfect accord of your sentiments and your charity you send up a chorus of praises to Christ. Let each one join in this chorus; then, in the harmony of concord, you will reach the tone of God through your own anointing and with one voice in Jesus Christ you shall sing the praise of the Father, who hearing you, will recognize the singing of his Son" (*Ep.* IV).

Just as Christ is the *tradition* of God, and the Apostles

31 Rousseau, *op. cit.*, p. 13.
32 B. Luykx, "De l'évêque," *Les Quest. Lit. Paroiss.*, XXXVII (1956), p. 196.

the tradition of Christ, the bishop, says Colson, "is for a specific place the *tradition* of Jesus Christ through the centuries."[33] The bishops are, in truth, the trustees of the word and life of Christ. This is guaranteed by the apostolic succession and by their communion with the bishop of Rome. The bishop embodies the true memory of the Church for a given generation and place; he is a living witness to Christ. For this reason we can say with Cyprian that a Church is "a people united to its bishop" (*Ep.* LXVI: VIII, 2-3), and also in the same letter: "The bishop is in the Church and the Church in the bishop." For the same reason Ignatius wrote in one of his epistles: "It is your whole Church which I contemplate in the person of your bishop" (*Trall.* I: 1).

Of the three classes of powers that theologians attribute to the Apostles (pastors, founders, and members of a college) only the pastoral and collegiate powers have been transmitted to their successors; the pastoral powers to every bishop, and the collegiate powers to the college of bishops united to the Roman pontiff. The extraordinary powers of the Apostles as founders of the Church ended with their death.

In his diocese the bishop is doctor of the faith, chief priest of the liturgy and shepherd of the flock entrusted to him. He is moreover a mediator of truth and life for one purpose: that of continuing Jesus Christ in the Church.[34]

2) *Primacy and episcopate*

In the opinion of the Apostolic Fathers "all the bishops are merely one in the spirit of Jesus Christ" (Ignatius, *Ep.* III:2); "through Christ's institution there is only one Church extended among many mem-

33 Colson, "Qu'est-ce qu'un diocèse?" *op. cit.*, p. 475.
34 Cf. Msgr. Guerry, *L'évêque* (Paris, 1954), pp. 15-35.

bers" (Cyprian, *Ep.* LXVI: VIII, 3). "The episcopate," continues Cyprian, is one and indivisible. The episcopal dignity is one and each bishop participated equally in possessing a part of it yet without division of the whole" (*De Unit.* 5). This is to say, "every bishop is a bishop not *individually* (although he is so personally) but rather *collegiately,* in solidarity with the sum of the episcopate."[35]

From the very successors of the Apostles on down, the bishops have always been conscious of their unity. They frequently exchanged correspondence among themselves in an effort to test their own opinions; they intervened in the naming of bishops for neighboring sees. and often met with other bishops of the same region, with such meetings presided over by one from a diocese of apostolic origin. Nevertheless, their unity did not operate on a regional basis but from the beginning of the Church was totally catholic, i.e., universal. Peter and his successors have been the visible center of this unity. "In the same way that the unity of the diocese is embodied in the bishop, the efficacious symbol of its unity, so also, the unity in the spirit of Jesus Christ of the episcopal college, the visible framework of the Church, is embodied in a visible image, an efficacious symbol of this unity: the Roman pontiff."[36]

The pope is the local and universal bishop. He must be a local bishop so that he embodies the Church in a given place; he must be universal so that there is a bond of union for all the episcopal communion, so that there exists a central point in the Church's apostolicity. The bishops are not representatives of the pope but instead authentic *colleagues* "united to him in the unity of the

35 Colson, *op. cit.,* p. 479.
36 *Ibid.,* pp. 480-481.

universal episcopate, of which he is the bond of union."[37] Thus the Code of Canon Law attributes to every bishop an "ordinary jurisdiction," although "subject to the authority of the Roman pontiff" (c. 329); it is a power rooted in the office, not the person. And for the same reason the pope has "the supreme and full power of jurisdiction in the universal Church" (c. 218:1).

Even though the bishop can exist without the priests, without bishops a pope is inconceivable, for the pope must necessarily be a bishop. Rahner says: "There is nothing that the bishops can do which is not likewise possible for the pope, and everything which they can do, they do it under subordination to the pope."[38] A bishop who breaks his unity with Rome is no longer the local embodiment of the universal and apostolic Church, but instead a private party who has received the episcopal function and who, because of its sacramentality, retains its powers although lacking the legitimate use of them.

The primacy exists because the universal Church is one; the episcopate exists because the universal Church appears in each local church by virtue of the faith and the mysteries of the faith. "In the same sense and degree that the universal Church exists in the local church, there also exists in this individual church the power of order and jurisdiction."[39] The more intensely the essence of the universal Church appears in his diocese, the more a bishop in communion with Rome embodies the universal Church in his local church. Therefore one cannot conceive of a bishop who would not proclaim the Word, solemnly celebrate the Eucharist in Pontifical Mass, and

37 *Ibid.*, p. 481; cf. A. Briva, "Colegio Episcopal e Iglesia Particular," *Seminario Conciliar* (Barcelona, 1959), p. 25.
38 K. Rahner, "Primat und Episkopat," *op. cit.*, p. 325.
39 *Ibid.*, p. 332.

anxiously tend his diocesan flock. To the degree that this is done, the Church will be present there.[40]

From this, one deduces the importance that episcopal pastoral activity has for all parishes. There is no doubt that, although they cannot be radically separated, the function is not the same as a charism. But there will always be a pastoral danger in lack of coordination between the episcopal apostolate for a diocese and that which certain or all pastors develop privately for their local communities, especially when this is done without the knowledge and approval of the bishop.

"If the bishop can impart to this local church all the mystery of the universal Christ," declares Guerry, "it is because, as a member of the episcopal college, successor of the Apostolic College, he is in communication with the mystery of the universal Church and in communication with all the other members of the body of bishops through his union with the Supreme Pontiff. How admirable is the unity of the episcopate. In the Church of Jesus everything is under the sign of unity, everything is marked by unity. Since there is but one Church, because there was but one Body of Christ, likewise there is but one episcopate since there was only one Apostolic College of the Twelve."[41]

In summary, as Paul stated: "One Lord, one faith, one Baptism; one God and Father of all , who is above all, and throughout all, and in us all" (Eph. 4:5-6).

3) *Episcopate and priesthood*

The most ancient and authentic tradition supports the unity of the *sacerdotium.* The controversy over the

40 Cf. M. Useros, "La parroquia, tema de la Ecclesiologia y del Derecho Canónico," *Revista Española de Derecho Canónico,* XVII (1962), 191-208.

41 Guerry, *op. cit.,* pp. 53-54.

sacramental character of the episcopate is very old, but despite the fact that most post-Trent theologians have supported such a sacramental character, there still have been some recent voices, such as Father Boyer's, which were not wholly in agreement.[42] The Council of Trent clearly declared that, in the line of order, the priesthood has three degrees—episcopate, priesthood, and diaconate—and that in this same line the episcopate is superior to the priesthood. The Council left it to the theologians to decide whether this superiority is through divine or ecclesiastical right. The Code (c. 108:3), summing up traditional doctrine, declared that "in virtue of divine institution, the holy hierarchy, in order of rank, consists of bishops, priests, and ministers."

One difficulty in differentiating the episcopate from the priesthood is to be found in the three pontifical bulls of Boniface IX (1400), Martin V (1427), and Innocent III (1489) by which the faculty of ordaining subdeacons, deacons, and priests was conferred upon Cistercian abbots not endowed with episcopal character.[43] These documents seem to be proven and accepted by everyone. Explanations are varied and as yet no clear solution has been reached. For some observers, the difference between episcopate and priesthood does not stem from divine right; that is, their powers are equal although those of the priesthood are limited by the Church's will. Others maintain that they are different by divine right, in that the episcopate is a true sacrament which gives, along with power, the grace proper to the consecration.[44]

42 "Nature et position du sacerdoce," *Nouv. Rev. Théol.* LXXVI (1954), April-May.

43 Y. M.-J. Congar, "Faits, problèmes et reflexions à propos du pouvoir d'ordre et de rapports entre le presbyterat et l'episcopat," *La Maison-Dieu,* XIV (1948), pp. 107-128.

44 Guerry, *op. cit.,* p. 127.

The one thing certain is that they are two different degrees within a single priesthood: that of the bishops is complete while that of the ordinary priests ("sacerdotes secundi ordinis") is reduced to essentials, limited and subordinate. According to the apostolic constitution of Pius XII (Nov. 30, 1944), "it is absolutely beyond a doubt and solidly established by widespread practice that the bishop is the minister of episcopal consecration." The fact that a priest in certain circumstances may be able to ordain priests cannot lead us to conclude that he can do the same as a bishop; it is a fact that no priest has ever consecrated a bishop. The consecration of a bishop takes on an extraordinary solemnity in the liturgy. Although it may be proved by the previous mentioned bulls that episcopal consecration does not add a sacramental *power,* it would be very difficult to prove that it does not add a sacramental *grace,* which after all is the distinctive sign of sacramentality.[45]

The origin of the episcopate and presbyterate is obscure. We have seen that in the second and third centuries the Eucharist was celebrated only by the bishop. It soon became clear that this practice was unsatisfactory for pastoral reasons. St. Leo set the rule for the Eucharist to be celebrated several times in a basilica if the latter were too small to hold all the faithful; the priesthood was thus already multiplied in the late third century. According to the distinguished Protestant scholar Gregory Dix, the presbyter had a jurisdictional function in the *presbyterium* whereas that of the deacon was liturgical. Reasons of necessity forced the Christians to have recourse to the priests for religious services during Diocletian's persecution. Actually, it was only from the fifth century on that they celebrated the Eucharist regu-

45 *Ibid.,* cf. A. Briva, *op. cit.,* pp. 66-67.

larly.[46] This opinion is the one generally held by Protestants.

In reality, our Lord handed over to the Church the substance of the sacraments but left it up to her own free choice how to best organize them with her canonical powers; the only exceptions are Baptism and the Eucharist. Today we find that the bishop differs from the simple priest because of his episcopal power, which is by divine right. With respect to the power of orders, the bishop is a full priest and with respect to power of jurisdiction, a direct successor of the Apostles. The priest who presides over a local community within a particular church is a *cooperator episcopi,* with an exercised power below that of the bishop, as we shall see later on.

In brief, we can say that the diocese is the local church, visibly represented by its bishop, the image of the Father, representative of Christ, and colleague of the Bishop of Rome, under whose authority he tends the flock that the Church has entrusted to him. The diocese is composed of small Christian communities, presided over by a priest of second rank, in which the Church lives and acts. However, it does not have the complete fullness of the mother or local church where the bishop pontificates, since only his priesthood, because it is apostolic, is full.

3. The Parish, Local Eucharistic Community

a) Modern pastoral thought

In the renovation of its pastoral life as well as in the attention it is attracting among modern theologians, the parish is enjoying a unique situation today.

Two fundamental causes have effectively intervened

46 Congar, "Faits, problèmes . . ." *op. cit.,* p. 123; there Congar mentions Dix's main works.

in the renewal of the parish. The first has stemmed from theology and more specifically ecclesiology, while the second originated in pastoral work and, concretely, religious sociology.

The first thoughts on the Church's communal and mystical aspects grew out of the theological movement of the Tübingen school, which introduced romanticism into Catholic theology. Sailer and, above all, Möhler were seeking a synthesis of objective data with subjective expression, of the systematic with the historical, of dogma with psychology, of doctrine with action. Journet calls Möhler and Newman "sensitive antennas" of modern ecclesiology. This movement was continued by the neoclassicists Franzelin and Scheeben, to the point where it is very widespread today.

While nineteenth-century rationalism followed a path toward intuitive metaphysics, and individualism tended toward a communitarian viewpoint, two young German theologians, Guardini and Neundörfer, attracted attention after the First World War with their declaration of the communal sense of the Church. They had been preceded in this field by Pilgran's noteworthy work in 1860. Since then there has been no end to profound works on the Church by the best theologians, from which we have inherited many theological and pastoral concepts of the parish.

Similarly, from 1931 on—beginning with a famous manifesto by Gabriel Le Bras, and above all since the end of the Second World War—there has been an uninterrupted succession of socio-ecclesial studies of parish and diocesan structures. The pastoral application of this new science was born of a dominant preoccupation with the great problem of dechristianization. There was an urgent need to know the forces of Catholicism in a universal examination of conscience, and the study unit was the parish.

The modern ecclesiological movement added mystical consideration to the visible structure of the Church as a perfect society, and modern jurists and sociologists added the socio-religious consideration to the frequently rigid and unchanging juridical aspect which prevailed among canonists.

And a last, more particular cause resulted in the parish occupying the focus of German theological-pastoral thought, which was the most advanced in Europe during the period between the two World Wars. This cause was the almost exclusive reduction of the Church in Germany to parish life during the Nazi period. It was precisely then that the great discussions began.

1) *"Ecclesiola in ecclesia"*

The first controversy developed around the very essence of the parish. Linked to this debate were others, such as that of the *Pfarrprinzip* (the parish principle) which was the matter of whether all care of souls should be on a parish level.

In 1925 the parish care of souls was just one more theme among many others.[47] But ten years later, shortly before the war, it had become almost the only theme of German pastoral thought of the time, which was marked by a deep restlessness.[48]

A. Wintersig began the dialogue in 1925.[49] "Before

47 *Paulus*, II (1925), p. 367; cf. J. Homeyer, "Die Erneuerung des Pfarregedankes. Eine bibliographische Übersicht," *Die Pfarre* (Freiburg im Br., 1956), p. 140.

48 *Paulus*, XIII (1936), pp. 339-343.

49 A. Wintersig, "Pfarrei und Mysterium," *Jahrb. f. Liturgiew.*, V (1925), pp. 136-143. Fr. tr.: "Le réalisme mystique de la paroisse," *La Maison-Dieu*, VIII (1946), pp. 15-26. Fr. tr. cited here because of greater accessibility.

being a social fact," he wrote, "the parish presents us with a supernatural reality. It is not first of all an object of sociological research" (p. 15). He maintained that the parish could only be studied theologically, with the point of departure being the incarnation of the Logos and the fact that the Church is the Mystical Body of Christ. Naturally, the parish is not a Church in the full sense of the word as is the diocese, he claimed, but essentially ". . . it is an integral cell which reflects and unites as in a microorganism the life of all the Body of Christ, which is the Church" (p. 16). The parish is the image of the universal Church. The baptismal font in the parish church is the maternal womb of the parish community; thus, the consecration of the font is first in a logical order. In this sense "each Christian finds the Church in a concrete parish" (p. 16). Through Confirmation received in the parish, the baptized person enters the great diocesan community, acquiring the fullness of baptismal character and active participation in the general priesthood of the faithful.

This sacramental initiation culminates in the celebration of the Eucharist on Sundays and feast days when the life of the Christian community is renewed through the actualization of Christ's redemption under the veil of sacramental mystery. "Through the sacrament of matrimony, day-to-day temporal life becomes directly adapted to sanctification in Christ" (p. 21). The practice of charity should be linked with the Eucharist. The loss of this relationship, claims Wintersig, has led to an outbreak of a variety of supra-parochial charitable institutions. "Authentic Christian charity, however, is agape and as such ought to be essentially and organically integrated into the life of the parish" (p. 23). The same could be said of education. "The most painful social problems ought to give way before the *sui generis* dynamism of the parish" (p. 26). Although rural surroundings are ideal for the parish, the urban environment can be impregnated by the city parish. "A church's altar symbolizes Christ: it is the cornerstone, the vital spot which unites the husband and wife through the graces of the mystery" (p. 26). The altar is fundamentally parochial because the work of redemption is carried out almost completely in the parish.

Following this typically liturgical concept of Wintersig's came others in the same vein by K. Jacobs, J. Pinsk, Pius Parsch, and M. Schurr.[50] Pius Parsch, writing in 1934, stated that "the parish's real problem lies in a living parochial community."[51] "The parish is *Ecclesia*," he said, "the Church in miniature, a concrete manifestation of the Church for each Christian" (p. 14). After stating this, he went on to a consideration of the Church as the Body of Christ. Since the essential thing for the Church is the transmission of life or grace, this will be the first mission of the parish: its sacramental life, which cannot be achieved without community. The pastor is the head, the father of the parish family, Christ in his community. The community is the body. The pastor is liturgist before being a missionary. In short, says Parsch, "the dogmatic fundamental of the living parish family is the Mystical Body of Christ. The two basic pillars which the building rests on are divine life and the community. The parish family should reconstruct

50 Cf. K. Jacobs, "Das Mysterium als Grundgedanke der Seelsorge," *Bonner Zeitschr. f. Theol. u. Seels.*, 1928, pp. 364-371; J. Pinsk, "Die religiöse Wirklichkeit von Kirche Diözese und Pfarrei," *Der Katolische Gedanke*, VI (1933), pp. 337-344; P. Parsch, "Die Pfarre als Mysterium," *Die Lebendige Pfarrgemeinde*, Seelsorger-Sonderheft, 1934, pp. 13-33; M. Schurr, "Die Übernatürliche Wirklichkeit der Pfarrei," *Benediktinische Monatsschrift*, XIX (1937), pp. 81-106.

51 Parsch, *op. cit.*, p. 13.

itself inside church at the altar and outside the church in the parish house" (p. 33). For Schurr, the parish is "the very representation and achievement of the Church" (p. 105). "It is a supernatural reality, Christ in his fullness, Christ dedicated. . . . It is the first and most profound ecclesial community of sacrifice, prayer, and life" (p. 105). It is an *"Ecclesiola in Ecclesia"* (p. 89).

2) *A juridical reality*

In 1934, after the Nazi suppression of all inter-parish association in Germany, the question arose: "Is the parish community the only form of Christian community?"[52] "The meaning of parish community is awakening again," wrote Jungmann in 1936, "thus pushing into the foreground the union of all neighboring believers among themselves, their inter-relation according to their natural classes, their spontaneous disposition for the local task of healing souls. Any other form of Christian organization derives its natural source from that life. The life of the universal Church cannot be better constructed than with each live cell of the individual Church."[53] Actually, the parish at that time received not only the main share of pastoral attention and activity but the brunt of theological thought on the treatment of souls as well. An exposition of this school of thought is to be found in C. Noppel's book, *Die neue Pfarrei* (Freiburg im Br., 1939).

The canonist Oswald von Nell-Breuning reacted against this theological-liturgical type of approach in 1947. He defended the thesis that the study of the parish is a task for the canonist and that it is "extremely danger-

52 K. Zimmermann, "Ist die Pfarrgemeinde die einzige christliche Gemeinschaftsform?" *Deutsches Volk*, Sept. 1934.

53 J. A. Jungmann, *Die Frohbotschaft und unsere Glaubensverkündigung* (Ratisbonne, 1936), p. 116.

ous"[54] to consider the parish as an "Ecclesiola in Ecclesia," according to Schurr's definition. This concept of Nell-Breuning ran into opposition since it was so unilaterally canonistic. In the general mind the parish was a mystical community on the one hand and the first and most adequate place for the healing of souls on the other.[55]

In 1949 L. Siemer also challenged the point of view advanced by Wintersig, but this time from a theological angle. He vigorously declared that "a diocese, and much less a parish, is not the Christ that mysteriously survives, since only in the overall Church does the Lord go on living mysteriously with full strength. Therefore, to consider the parish as *ecclesiola* is not only disconcerting but false."[56] Nor can the matter of liturgy be brought up, he adds, since the complete, full liturgist is not the pastor but rather the bishop. "In the clearest possible way the presence of the Mystical Body of Christ and the concrete form of the living community of faith, worship, and love are seen when priests and faithful join in the community of prayer and the breaking of bread. And this occurs in exactly the same degree in the parish community as in any other" (p. 46).

Karl Rahner wrote in 1948 that "in the present healing of souls, parish pastoral work is not the only activity."[57] Besides the territorial dimension there are

54 O. V. Nell-Breuning, "Pfarrgemeinde, Pfarrfamilie, Pfarrprinzip," *Trierer Theol. Zeitschr.*, LVI (1947), 285.

55 Cf. J. Höffner, "Nochmals das Pfarrprinzip," *Trierer Theol. Zeitschr.*, LVII (1948), 236-239; J. Homeyer, "Die Erneuerung . . ." *op. cit.*, p. 34.

56 L. Siemer, "Pfarrfamilie und Ecclesiola," *Die Neue Ordnung*, III (1949), 44.

57 K. Rahner, "Friedliche Erwägungen über das Pfarrprinzip," *Schriften zur Theologie*, Einseideln, II (1955), 325. This work was first published in *Zeitschr. f. Kathol. Theol.*, LXX (1948), 169-198.

many others in which it is possible to conceive of a genuine pastoral activity; history demonstrates that the parish apostolate has not been the only one. Furthermore, everyone has in the Church the right to form a part of the community of his choice (p. 320). For these three reasons, Rahner admits to apostolic forms different from the parochial apostolate.

3) *A missionary community*

At the end of World War II the French came onto the parish scene with two pastoral congresses, held in Besançon (1946) and Lille (1948). In the first one, under the general theme "Paroisse, chretienté communautaire et missionnaire," the dominant preoccupation with community and missionary action clearly rose to the surface. Until then the juridical concept of the parish had prevailed in the Latin countries; the concept and even the reality of missions thus proved to be new. The book by Godin and Daniel, *France pays de mission?* had appeared in 1943 and stirred up profound interest. Along with Michonneau's *Paroisse, communauté missionnaire* (1945) and F. Boulard's *Problèmes missionnaires de la France Rurale* (1946) it formed a classic trilogy in the new sociological and missionary movement. The theology of this important new pastoral aspect was supplied by Cardinal Suhard in his three well-known pastoral letters of 1947, 1948, and 1949: "Essor oü déclin de l'Eglise," "Le sens de Dieu" and "Le Prêtre dans la cité."

Godin's book had amounted to a strong attack against the traditional parish, and the newly emerging works of religious sociology underlined the gravity of the situation. The French, following a more sociological path, reached the same conclusion as the Germans, who pursued a typically theological one: it was urgently necessary to revitalize the parish.

The positive reaction came with the congresses at Besançon and Lille, and the Michonneau book. The contribution of French parish thought of the time was a consideration of the sociological reality in which the parish lived, an aspect often forgotten beyond the Rhine. The true parish, as M. Augros says, is "wherever there is a human community where Christ can become incarnate and diffuse his spirit, which is at one and the same time a spirit of fraternal charity and a spirit of religion."[58] The parish is "a sociological reality made divine and on the road to divinization" (p. 18). It is therefore not solely a center of worship and place of sanctification. It is the universal Church established in one certain point in space, a point where there is a sector of human life, a center of life to establish communion with God in Christ (p. 18). It is the Church in one point in space, the Church in one of its cells.

Both aspects, the sociological and the missionary, joined forces in the thinking of this first French congress. At the close of the sessions Cardinal Feltin published some reflections in *La Maison-Dieu,* calling the parish "a diffusion center for supernatural life in the bosom of humanity."[59] While it is a living community, open and traditional, it is also a community that prays, a fraternal community, and a missionary community.

Yves Congar's contribution was outstanding at the 1948 Lille congress, whose theme was "Structures sociales et pastorale paroissiale." He picked up the train of German thought begun with Wintersig and, after weighing the efforts of those theologians who had gone beyond mere canonical or administrative considerations, ex-

58 M. Augros, "La paroisse dans l'Eglise in 1946," *Paroisse, chrétienté communautaire et missionaire* (Paris, 1946), p. 18.

59 Card. Feltin, "Quelques réflexions sur la paroisse," *La Maison-Dieu,* IX (1947), 105.

pressed the opinion that such a concept is too narrow for expressing an adequate theology of the parish.[60] He felt they saw the Church almost exclusively as a community of worship; this is an essential consideration but not the only one or the complete one. It is necessary to add to the picture the social element of human life.

To Congar's way of thinking, the parish was born because of the pastoral convenience it affords. It suits the needs of a group of men living in the same neighborhood because it provides the opportunity to undertake jointly the basic tasks of life (p. 51). Unity of residence and the existence of communities of neighbors are primary, natural, social realities. He recalled the fact that the parish has been compared to the family, and the diocese to the city. Indeed, he continued, the Church is both family and city: family when considered as parish and city when studied as diocese. "Basically the Church, from beginning to end, is built according to the image and likeness of trinitarian society and follows the dual principle of hierarchy and communication" (p. 58). But there are also things in the Church that stem from the human and social planes. "The parish is the means of generation and formation of the Christian person" (p. 153), and of his basic Christian formation. Congar disputed Michonneau's thesis, maintaining that the parish does not impose *spirituality.* It should contribute the basic element within a family environment. Its main function is "forming and preparing Christian souls *sine addito* in ordinary life for their concrete responsibilities" (p. 57). Considering the parish as a family, the priest is a teacher of Christian life; considering it as community, the priest lives in the midst of men and with men. "The Church community is living and active when its

60 Y. M.-J. Congar, "Mission de la paroisse," *Structures Sociales et Pastorale Paroissiale* (Paris, 1948), 49.

existence is sustained by the apostolic ministry of the word and the sacraments of the faith" (p. 60). In a word the parish's job, according to Congar, is to "form persons who happen to live in the same district and are joined by everyday mutual aid in a *sine addito* Christian life" (p. 62).

4) *A cell of the Mystical Body*

In the meantime and especially in Germany, the liturgical movement had taken hold. In its first stage, at the end of World War I, the liturgy was lived by a small circle of intellectuals; later on its dynamism was transmitted to young people and finally, in a third phase, it spread to parish communities. The biblical and liturgical renewal movements have been extraordinarily fruitful for parish pastoral activity, since the life of a parochial community should be based on Scripture and worship. Before the last war the Viennese Pastoral Institute sponsored a strong parish biblical and liturgical movement. In 1942 and 1943, K. Borgmann, in collaboration with outstanding liturgists and theologians like Guardini, Jungmann, Walter, Gunkel, Kirchgässner, Rahner, Pascher, Tilmann and others, published two works of great importance in grafting the recent liturgical advances onto the parish's task of tending souls.[61]

In 1943 a widespread popular and scientific liturgical movement began with the creation of the *Centre de Pastorale Liturgique*,[62] which sponsored numerous liturgical and parish workshops and began publication of the excellent magazine *La Maison-Dieu.*

61 "Volksliturgie und Seelsorge. Ein Werkbuch zur Gestaltung des Gottesdienstes in der Pfarrgemeinde," Kolmar, 1942; "Parochia, Handreichung für die Pfarrseelsorge" (Kolmar, 1943).

62 Cf. A.-G. Martimort, "Quince años de pastoral litúrgica en Francia," *Comunidad cristiana parroquial* (Madrid, 1959), 199-221.

In Italy the parish has been attracting renewed attention since 1952. The magazine *Quaderni Tabor* (1952, n. 3), *Vita sociale* (1952, n. 9), *La Scuola Cattolica* (1953, Nov.-Dec.) and *Orientamenti Pastorali* (1954, May-Sept.) devoted special issues to the parish, echoing all the German and French pastoral thought. Italian pastoral theologians accepted an idea about the parish which went beyond mere canonical limits. L. Nanni offered a magnificent résumé of the history of the parish in *La Scuola Cattolica,* along with another, no less valuable study on parish sociology by A. Rimoldi. In 1954 the *IV Settimana Nazionale di Aggiornamento Pastorale* was held in Bologna with this theme: "La Parrochia—Aspetti pastorali e missionari" (Milan, 1955). Cardinal Lercaro defined the parish as "a live and vital cell of the Mystical Body of Christ" (p. 51), along the lines of German thinking. At the same congress G. Ceriani defended the dual aspect of the parish—mystical and juridical, social and communal—as being *societas fidelium* and *familia Dei.* From the example of the Eucharist, wherein each consecrated particle contains Christ completely, he deduced that the parish is part of, and yet contains all of the Church. He emphasized the influence of the social factor, which ought to be ranked with the territorial one.

Canadian thought was moving along similar lines in 1953, when a Social Week was held devoting more attention to the juridical and social aspects than to mystical or theological ones. An important letter was sent to the participants of this discussion week by Archbishop Montini, then Pius XII's Pro-Secretary of State,[63] in which he said that the parish is "the smallest part of the sole and universal flock entrusted by the Lord to Peter. Under

63 *Col. Enc. y Doc. Pont.* (Madrid, 1955), pp. 1464-1465; French text: *La Maison-Dieu,* XXXVI (1953), 9-13.

the authority of a responsible priest, who has received from his bishop the charge of caring for souls, it is the first community of Christian life in the Church of Jesus Christ" (p. 7). It is before anything else a "home of religious life and missionary expansion" (p. 8), a "truly living and active cell of the Body of Christ" (p. 8), and a "community built around faith, prayer, and charity" (p. 11).

5) *A local community of faith, worship, and charity*

Theological thinking on the parish was reaffirmed even more on the occasion of the pastoral workshops of Vienna in 1953. F.-X. Arnold began his lecture on the theology of the parish with a clarification of terms. The parish is a community that lives in a land that is not its own, he recalled; it is a pilgrim community. He later examined the juridical and theological aspects with a balanced judgment perhaps lacking in the prewar German thinkers. "The juridical aspect of the parish," he said, "testifies to its character as a member of the diocese besides manifesting its universality, objectivity, and capacity for giving to Christ, as well as the solidity and awareness of its action."[64] Based on Wikenhauser's work *Die Kirche als das mystische Leib Christi nach dem Apostel Paulus* (Münster, 1937), upon which almost all liturgists of the parish depend, he stated that "each local community, according to the Pauline concept, represents and takes part in the entire Church" (p. 96). "Whatever is valid about the Church for the diocese can likewise be said of the parish *per modum participationis*—that is, the parish participates in the spiritual fullness and Christological interaction of the universal Church even though it be subordinate and dependent to it" (p. 100).

64 F.-X. Arnold, *Glaubensverkündigung und Glaubensgemeinschaft* (Düsseldorf, 1955), pp. 92-93.

"It ought to be a community of faith, prayer and charity" (p. 101). Arnold admitted with Rahner that there are other apostolic dimensions besides the territorial one, but that it is precisely within the parish that faith, prayer, and charity find their first and most natural projection (p. 90).

A few years later, in 1956, a group of professors from Innsbruck returned to the same theme of the parish. Especially outstanding was the work of Karl Rahner, who went deepest of all into the theological essence of the parish by connecting the celebration of the Eucharist —essence of the Church—to the principle of local community.[65] He began with the supposition that "the Church as an event [*Ereignis*] is necessarily a local community" (p. 29), since "its most intense event is the celebration of the Eucharist" (p. 32) which is essentially linked to a local area. "The parish does not operate through a participation in the universal Church's space but rather through a concentration of the Church according to its own capacity for being an event" (p. 33). From these principles he deduces his second thesis: "the parish is the first actualization of the Church as event" (p. 34). Naturally, there are other Christian communities, even local ones, but "the parish is the first actualization of the Church as event because its eucharistic celebration is linked primarily and naturally to local areas" (p. 35).

Also outstanding in this cycle of lectures was the contribution of H. Kahlefeld on community life in the New Testament. It concluded with several conclusions that magnificently summarize all of German thinking on the subject of the parish.[66]

65 K. Rahner, "Zur Theologie der Pfarre," *Die Pfarre* (Freiburg, 1956), pp. 27-39.

66 H. Kahlefeld, "Das Leben der Gemeinde nach dem Neuen Testament," *Die Pfarre* (Freiburg, 1956), pp. 64-66.

1. The parish community is the Holy Church, the people of God, the salvific community of the Messiah, the family of the baptized living in one specific area, in the midst of the human community of the *Polis.*

2. This community is the bearer of salvation for all men with whom Christians form the *Polis.* It gives a public manifestation founded by God and consequently bears a corresponding responsibility.

3. The community lives not only in the assembly place (the church or places of worship) but in the homes of all Christians as well.

4. The celebration of the Eucharist is the most profound source and the highest manifestation of the life of the family of God.

5. The now-neglected "Supper of Charity" (agape) ought to find its continuation in the community members' charitable care of the poor, and extra-liturgically in community gatherings full of a great spirit of brotherhood.

6. On the vigils of Sundays or holy days a liturgy of the word should be celebrated with a reading of pericopes chosen from the Old and New Testaments, followed by a biblical homily and a community prayer full of spirit, so that everything serves to nourish the Christians' faith.

7. The pastor is the father of families in his community. As shepherd of his flock he takes care of order in community life and attends to everyone's spiritual and corporal needs, besides being responsible for the conservation and successive passing along of the storehouse of faith and the appropriate celebration of the mysteries.

8. There are various functions in the liturgical assembly subordinate to the building up of the community and to worship, each according to its own kind. Paul

says that all are means of action of the Spirit of Christ, which is to say they are charismatic functions.

In 1957 J. Wagner wrote a profound article on the parish community that attempted to center the matter theologically.[67] Wagner felt that "the community principle as such is of divine will" (p. 219). Alongside the liturgical *actio* (the Mass) should be put the other apostolic actions; the motto or slogan was no longer "liturgy alone" but rather "pastoral activity from the altar," since although "worship is the Church's holiest mission," it is not the only one. For this reason it is necessary to speak of liturgy, deaconship, and martyrdom. "Worship and action, liturgy, deaconship, and martyrdom are charisms that the divine Founder has bestowed on his Church through the Pneuma and which he has granted perpetually. These charisms are meant for each other also; they pervade one another, live off one another and are directed toward one another. Together they build up the community. Even though worship—the liturgy—occupies first place, the community cannot be deprived of the rest" (p. 225).

D. Grasso has gathered together the opinions expressed about the parish since the subject was first undertaken by Wintersig.[68] Basically he follows the process described by J. Homeyer in 1956 on the occasion of the Innsbruck conference in which various theologians and liturgists took part. Grasso tends toward a middle-of-the-road position. He does state that "an extension to the parish of the properties of Church and diocese is both legitimate and necessary" (p. 304), but one can only speak of a relationship properly speaking "if one can

67 J. Wagner, "Kult und Aktion im Aufbau der Pfarrgemeinde," *Liturgisches Jahrbuch*, VII (1957), 215-225.

68 D. Grasso, "Osservazioni sulla teologia della parrochia," *Gregorianum*, XL (1959), 297-314.

succeed in demonstrating that the parish's origin from the diocese has, apart from contingent and certain special factors, been due to an intrinsic pressing demand of ecclesial action that the diocese or community gathered around the bishop could not satisfy" (p. 305). He points out that the expression *ecclesiola* has the danger of making the parish appear independent from the diocese. Nevertheless, the parish was born historically as a prolongation of the diocese. In this sense the pastor is a prolongation, a "cooperator" of the bishop. Grasso concludes that "the parish can be the object of theology as a prolongation of the diocese" (p. 311).

The first Spanish contribution of any consequence to parochial thought was made by P. Bidagor's *La "Iglesia propia" en España* (Rome, 1933), a weighty historic-canonical study. Along with this basic work, mention should also be made of J. Fernández Alonso's documented study, *La cura pastoral en la España romano-visigótica* (Rome, 1955). Both works have opened up horizons for Spanish pastoral thought through the ever-valuable lessons of history.

Actually, the first Spanish work to treat the pastoral problem of the parish along modern lines was a book by the present bishop of Vitoria, the Most Rev. F. Peralta, entitled *La estructura moderna de la parroquia en sus lineas fundamentales* (Zaragoza, 1949). However, until the Zaragoza Study Weeks, the parish theme had scarcely occupied the attention of thinkers and theologians at all. In 1953 Msgr. S. Beguiristain published a book called *Por esos pueblos de Dios* which made a strong impression on the younger clergy at whom it was aimed. This book was an optimistic treatment of pastoral work in the parish, without any critical intent and written in a novelized, poetic form. Using pontifical texts, Andrés Avelino Esteban wrote an interesting study called *El estado mayor del párroco* (Madrid, 1956) which was full of profitable instruction.

In 1957 Archbishop Casimiro of Madrid-Alcalá, who was then Archbishop of Zaragoza, organized a diocesan or interdiocesan Study Week in preparation for the national Study Week. The contributions and papers read at the meeting, which were gathered together into a volume called *La parroquia, esa vieja novedad,*[69] admittedly "vary a great deal in their style and compactness," declared Archbishop Morcillo. "All of them, however, proclaimed the need to renew the pastoral activity of our parishes and none failed to mention some change which could be made in such a renewal" (p. 19). The themes chosen were perhaps too ambitious and theologically they undoubtedly surpassed the abilities of the participants.

The first National Parish Study Week, celebrated a few months later in 1958, had a twofold advantage over the preceding meeting. For one thing the themes were simplified, although the general subject remained "The Power of Sanctifying, Teaching, and Governing." Furthermore, preparation by participants was in general more detailed and documented.[70] The congress was panoramic in character since, as Archbishop Morcillo observed in the Prologue, it was "the first time that the parish was to be completely unfolded before more than a thousand delegates from all over Spain and made the subject of contemplation and study by those wanting to discover its beauty and examine the future in store for it" (p. 4).

To Bishop Miranda, Auxiliary Bishop of Toledo, the

69 *La parroquia, esa vieja novedad* (Madrid: Euroamérica, 1948), 518 pp.
70 *Comunidad cristiana parroquial* (Madrid: Euroamérica, 1959), 598 pp.

parish was "a small organic unit of the Mystical Body of Christ . . . an organic member or cell of the diocesan (Church)" (p. 90), and "a true family of the children of God, a community made up of members united to Christ, a real Christian community" (p. 91).

In another session during the same week, in a talk rich with pastoral experience, Father Miguel Peinado called the parish "a portion of Christ's flock. It is the Church itself reduced to certain limits and specific circumstances. The whole Church is in the parish, even though its extension transcends the parish limits" (p. 305). That is, "it is a projection of the Mother Church tailored to our size" (p. 306), "a vital cell of that great social body which is our Holy Mother the Church" (p. 309). Msgr. Tabera, whose contribution to the congress dealt with the relations between the parish and religious orders, declared that "the parish is the authentic home of the Christian; in the parish Church and only in the parish Church does he find all the spiritual aids and means for his spiritual life . . . only in the parish does the Christian find what could be called the *complete schemata* of his Christian life *ab ortu nativitatis ad corporis sepulturam*" (p. 352).

Of all the papers presented at that congress the one that is of most interest to us is A. Hombría's work entitled "The Parish in the Teaching of the Church," which carefully collected everything that the popes, especially Pius XII, had said about the parish. While we do not intend to reproduce all the texts here, it would be well to recall that Pope Paul VI, then Cardinal Montini, called the parish a "truly live and active cell of the Mystical Body" (p. 68). According to Pius XII it is "the basic cell of ecclesiastical life" (p. 68) and in the mind of the Sacred Congregation of the Council "it is the first cell of the Mystical Body of Christ by which the faithful are united to their bishop and the pope and, through them, to God" (p. 68).

In late September of 1958, Archbishop Morcillo issued a pastoral letter on the theology of the parish which was a summary of all the pastoral thought of those two study weeks.[71] In order to define the parish he studied the mystical and canonical aspects, based on the three ecclesial actions. For one thing, "as an elementary organ of the Mystical Body of Christ, the parish is a Church of Christ in miniature with all the main notes and characteristics that distinguish the Church" (p. 9). Furthermore, "the parish and its true concept always mean relationship with the bishop and the diocesan Church" (p. 9). And finally it is a "hierarchical and organic community" (p. 10), "the primary and essential center of ecclesial life" (p. 9) and "a missionary community" (p. 11).

Since that first national parish week, two more have been held: the first in Seville, in May of 1960, with the theme "Penetration of the Parish in Various Environments," and the other in Barcelona two years later with the general title "Catholic Action and the Secular Apostolate in the Parish." With regard to the theology of the parish, these two weeks have merely followed the trend of earlier developments.[72]

Summing up the theological path that the parish has travelled these past few years, I take the liberty of quoting the conclusion of my paper "Toward a New Conception of the Parish" which was given at the Zaragoza

71 C. Morcillo, "Teología de la parroquia," *Pastoral Letter*, Zaragoza (Sept. 29, 1958). He cites the pages of the separate edition. Cf. this pastoral letter in his book, *La Iglesia Diocesana y sus parroquias* (Barcelona: Remanso, 1960).

72 The most important contribution is that of Msgr. N. Jubany, "La parroquia y la obra de evangelización," *Orbis Catholicus*, V (1962), 97-127.

Diocesan Week in September of 1957: "the parish is the local community of faith in Christ, born around its own baptismal font by virtue of the proclamation of the word. It celebrates and receives the Eucharist, is served by a priest and lives amid the human community in a missionary state, considering itself foreign and having no charter of citizenship there. The parish is a local community of love" (p. 78).[73]

6) *The parish and human communities*

Reflections on the parish are by no means over and done with, especially in the French-speaking countries.

In November, 1961, the first "Colloque Européen des Paroisses" gathered in Lausanne to deal with the problem of the parish from various pastoral angles. According to Ivan Daniel the parish has received beneficial influences from the liturgical, catechetical, sociological, apostolic, and even technical and administrative movements. Nevertheless, there is the problem of the parish's vitality as a missionary community because of its form and structure. "Geographical parishes," says Daniel, "correspond to the geographic dimension of human life. In today's big cities, parishes are not in themselves enough to insure the sanctification of modern man, who habitually and simultaneously lives in several 'milieux,' which quite often are very widely separated from each other."[74]

The missionary aspect of the parish has been dealt with by the editorial staff of the magazine *Parole et*

73 Cf. C. Floristán, "La parroquia en el pensamiento de la moderna pastoral," *Orbis Catholicus*, Aug.-Sept., III (1960), 110-124. An almost identical exposition of opinions has since been followed by V.G. de la Concha in his inaugural discourse, "La realidad teológica de la parroquia" (Oviedo: Metropolitan Seminary, 1960).

74 Y. Daniel, "Situation de la paroisse," in the minutes of the Ier Colloque Européen des Paroisses (Paris: 1962, pro ms.).

Mission (XX, Jan. 1963). According to this group, the "missionary parish" is that parish which in fact reaches non-believers and fallen-away Catholics (p. 23). In order to study this problem carefully, they subject the parish to a rigorous critical examination. Especially important is the work of Father Liégé; the noted French Dominican theologian uses as his point of departure the Church's mission, which is to say her dual poles of eucharistic and missionary activity. The parish should therefore be a eucharistic community and a missionary community, which means directed toward both God and man. Its missionary side demands that the parish be present among pagans and among the unbelieving masses as well as among its own parishioners. And this will be achieved, says Liégé, only when the parish ceases being self-sufficient and isolated, and opens itself up to the whole Church.

A subsequent look at the parish has been taken by another team of pastoral experts no less important than the *Parole et Mission* group: i.e., the staff of *Paroisse et Liturgie,* published at St. Andrew's Abbey in Belgium. "Religious sociology has underlined the deep transformation that has taken place in the modern parish, which is no longer in harmony, as was true in ages past, with the socio-cultural communities it embraces."[75] The most severe examination the parish has had to undergo is undoubtedly the one given it by the sociologists.[76]

For one thing, parish sociologists are studying community forms and religious membership from a psychosociological point of view, and furthermore they are

75 *La paroisse se cherche* (Bruges: 1963), p. 7.

76 Cf. E. Pin, "La Sociologie de la Paroisse" in Ier Colloque Européen des Paroisses, *op. cit.;* F. Houtart, "Pastorale missionaire et paroissiale dans les grandes villes," *Parole et Mission,* XX (1963), 55-78; "Sociologie de la paroisse comme assemblée eucharistique" in *La paroisse se cherche, op. cit.,* 111-125.

noting that social relationships, in our technical world, are less and less dependent upon the geographical area of residence. They all end up saying, some discreetly and others more openly, that the current parish, above all in the big cities, is not adapted to present sociological reality.

The current critique of the sociologist is thus added to that of the missionary. Unless pastoral theologians and in particular theologians of the parochial apostolate keep the real facts of the present situation in mind, there is a danger of formulating a theology that is not truly pastoral.[77]

Today's parish, and especially the urban one, is going to have to undergo a great pastoral transformation. It obviously will have to acquire one or another of these marks: eucharistic or liturgical and missionary or apostolic. This will happen when it becomes fully conscious of the fact that it is located within the true local community, which is the diocese, assuming that the diocese or local church takes on the dimensions of the universal Church.

b) Toward a complete vision of the parish

1) *Doctrinal suppositions*

From all the modern pastoral thought applied to the parish one can draw the important conclusion, formulated clearly by F.-X. Arnold: "Everything that can be deduced about the Church and the diocese is also valid for the parish *per modum participationis*."[78]

When speaking of the theology of the Church we have

77 Cf. the studies of J. Frisque in *La paroisse se cherche, op. cit.*, pp. 127-158.

78 F.-X. Arnold, "Zur Theologie der Pfarrei," *Glaubensverkündigung . . .," op. cit.*, p. 100.

already seen, although briefly, that the Church is visible and invisible, earthly and heavenly, temporal and eternal, present and eschatological, human and divine, active and contemplative, collective and individual, personal and suprapersonal. The parish also shares these dual aspects. It is obviously essential to seek the Church's ultimate roots—and consequently those of the parish—in its mystical nature. But this is not enough. In order to fully understand the Church, and thus the parish, it is important to keep in mind its visible aspect; the underlying reason for this is not the fact that man consists of a visible part (the body) and an invisible one (the soul), but rather it stems from the fundamental principle expressed in the Athanasian Creed of 447: "Our Lord Jesus Christ, the Son of God, is God and man: God, of the substance of the Father, begotten before the ages; man, of the substance of His mother, born into the world."[79] Man is not the model of Jesus but just the opposite: Jesus Christ, primogenitor of all creatures, is the model for all men.

In its visible aspect, the parish is a socio-religious structure with clearly defined contours and visible signs. Not all the visible part is essential to the parish, perhaps, but belongs to it at least in some way. Let us examine these visible appearances, not only on the basis of the data afforded us by the science of reason but also in the light of revelation. Let us thus pass from the visible to the invisible, from the historical to the eternal, from the human to the divine.

(a) *Revelation and situation*

There is no doubt that pastoral thought today is passing through an exceptional *Kairós* because of the deep

79 Denzinger 40.

and ceaseless renovation in the two areas to which its task can be reduced: revelation and situation. The Germans, untiring renovators that they are in matters of theology, have laid firm foundations; upon them, relying on biblical theology, they have built up a theology of history wherein the Christian concept of time plays a leading role. The French, preoccupied with the spiritual calamity of their country brought to light in the period following what they call *l'Ancien Regime,* have courageously determined to meet and solve their own particular situation. The rest of the countries are gravitating toward one of these two ways but it is truly consoling to observe how attentive the Germans are to French sociology, while the French are reacting in much the same way to German theological groundwork, where they can well relate their own valuable findings.

Obviously, theology is doctrinal and deductive: its points of departure are the Bible and tradition in the light of teaching, and it is not deduced from human events. But each time a new phenomenon occurs theology should be there on the spot to consider it from the point of view of its own special criteria of observation. In this sense theology either is current or else is not universal theology. It cannot be absent from the *vox temporis,* just as the voice of history will not be true unless listened to in the light of the *lumen aeternitatis.* Failure to make theology current is as dangerous as not meditating on current events theologically. What is more, for us there is such a bond between situation and revelation, between time and eternity, between divine and human nature, between *caro* and *Verbum,* that theology cannot follow a situation but must instead precede it.

The synthesis of revelation and situation must be theandric, so that the end product may be the effective care of souls. "Like *cooperatio* in the charitable movement between God and man," says Arnold, "the Church's care of souls is at once a collaboration with God and a service to man."[80] This demands two loyalties: one, in the form of a rule or standard, is loyalty to principles, to revelation, and to God; the other is loyalty to the situation, to real persons, to the communities of life. Said Cardinal Suhard: "The saint in his own being thus succeeds in harmonizing the two [loyalties]: he witnesses to the transcendence and the immanence of God, is at home in the two worlds of heaven and earth, is the man of God and a man among men."[81]

Pastoral theology has its practical nature since in the final analysis it is, in the light of revelation, a reflection of the care of souls. Its object consists in studying the Church's acts, which are theandric in character because they are aimed at building the Mystical Body of Christ. Jesus Christ, the Mediator between God and man, with His twin nature—human and divine—is the model of all ecclesial action. He lived in space, was subject to time, and in His human nature had a psychic and social constitution similar to that of man. The Church, the permanent incarnation of the Son of God, reproduces Jesus Christ.

Because of its dual aspect, transcendent and temporal, the Church is inconceivable without reference to the world. "Because she is the body of Christ," wrote Cardinal Suhard, "his incarnation in the history and the geography of the earth, the Church is first of all contingent. She belongs to a special time and place. . . . The world, for its own life, needs the Church; and the Church needs the world for her own development and comple-

80 F.-X. Arnold, *Grundsätzliches und Geschichtliches zur Theologie der Seelsorge* (Freiburg im Br., 1949), p. 51.

81 Card. Suhard, *The Meaning of God* (Notre Dame, 1963), p. 57.

tion."[82] Because of this relationship between the world and the Church, the theological sciences studying the Church's diverse aspects ought to have some contact with the sciences that analyze the factors of human life.

(b) *Pastoral preparation*

Although Augustine, on the basis of Scripture, radically divided the world into two cities—the *civitas Dei* (which for him was the *sancta Ecclesia*) and the *civitas impia* (which he often called the *civitas terrena*)—one can still note in his thinking a *tertium quid* which Journet called the "city of men."[83] On a spiritual plane and in the light of ultimate ends, the City of God is opposed to the City of the Devil, whose relations are governed by a law of opposition. If we consider intermediate ends for a moment, however, a third city can be detected. It is the City of Men, whose relationship with the Church is governed by a law of distinction which must be turned into a law of harmony. "Therefore there are three types of cities: the *City of God*, in which the Devil has no part; the *City of the Devil*, in whose sin God has no part, and the *City of Men*, sought after simultaneously by both higher cities."[84]

The City of God, by intervening in the City of Men, does attempt to make it more human but its real end, nevertheless, is not to humanize but rather to Christianize it. "The Church," said Pius XII, "does not evangelize

82 Card. Suhard, *Growth or Decline?* (Notre Dame, 1960), pp. 33-34, 36.

83 Ch. Journet, "Las tres ciudades: la de Dios, la del hombre y la del diablo," *Orbis Catholicus*, II (1958), 50; cf. H. I. Marrou, "Civitas Dei, civitas terrena: nun tertium quid?" *Studia Patristica*, v.64, tome II (Berlin, 1957), p. 348.

84 Journet, *op. cit.*, p. 53.

by civilizing but instead civilizes by evangelizing."[85] Accordingly, evangelization is at the same time civilization or humanzation; however, the reverse does not follow. But still and all Christianity is not authentic if it excuses itself from the pressing tasks of civilization. "A Christianity that sought refuge in the thought of heaven," wrote Cardinal Suenens, "in order to excuse itself from working for a better world, would annoy Christ. Unquestionably, the *quid hoc ad aeternitatem*—the reference to eternity—which forms an integral part of Christian life brands the temporal order once and for all with a coefficient of relativity."[86] Yet civilization is undergoing a slower development than Christianity, and although the job of civilization is indispensable, this does not mean that it is necessarily a prelude to Christianity.

The law of distinction between these two cities must come to be a law of harmony for the Christian, who is also a citizen of the kingdom of men. If man lives in sin, his work in the world can only be partially true, although it be humanly marvelous; if he lives in grace, his performance in the City of Man will have to be perfect, so that it be ideally Christian. One cannot give to God what is God's without giving to Caesar what is Caesar's. The only kind of apostolate is a flesh and blood one, just as there is no other kind of Christianity. "But there are two aspects of this apostolate," Cardinal Suenens has declared. "The first, the direct apostolate, proceeds from the religious to the human; the second, the indirect apostolate, goes from the human to the religious. A religious apostolate not connected with life is as unthinkable as a social apostolate without a religious basis."[87]

85 Pius XII, to the Versailles Social Week; cf. ref. in Leon-Joseph Cardinal Suenens, "La Iglesia en estado de missión," Sp. transl. (Bilbao, 1955), p. 48.
86 L. J. Suenens, *op. cit.*, p. 35.
87 *Ibid.*, p. 59.

There are, then, two points of reference for the citizens of the Kingdom of God, which is to say any Christian belonging to the Church: one is based in his own city, whose construction is brought about through the actions of the Church; the other is related to the city where Man lives. It would be incomplete to try to build the City of God without knowing the City of Man, even if one had sufficient faith in the vigor of the City of God's internal growth, just as it would be incomplete to attempt to build the Kingdom of God with only the knowledge or the enthusiasm of the earthly city. There are some citizens of the City of God—the priests—who are fundamentally dedicated to the final convergence of all ecclesial action, which is the celebration of the Eucharist. The rest of the citizens, the lay people, "collaborate with the hierarchy in the salvation of souls and work toward making the conditions of temporal life in the world suitable for facilitating the Church's redemptive mission."[88]

Pastoral theology, the theological science of ecclesial actions, directly observes the internal growth of the Kingdom of God; propaedeutical pastoral studies are the profane sciences that analyze the conditions in which the citizens of the earth live with regard to their Christianization. This pastoral science is *normative;* it comes to us from above, from revelation. The others are *indicative;* they originate down here on earth, from the situation. "Our point of departure," says J. F. Motte, "must be what is true in the faith and what is true in life."[89] It is precisely between these two poles—created by faith, which comes from God, and by life, as it is lived on earth—that the pastoral vocation operates. Its great aim is

88 Conclusions of the first Congress of the Lay Apostolate, mentioned in Suenens, *op. cit.*, p. 78.

89 J.-F. Motte and M. Dourmap, *Mission générale, oeuvre d'Eglise* (Paris, 1956), p. 88.

to enable human life to take on the brilliancy of divine life by means of the mysterious light of faith. "Missionary work," as Cardinal Suhard points out, "does not consist in finding out how the Church, such as it is, can become the model for the world but rather in discovering how the world, such as it is, can be raw material for the Church."

The person who sows the Gospel sows everywhere, but he *knows* that the farmland varies from one field to another (Luke 8:4-15); no one builds a tower without calculating the outlay necessary (Luke 14:28-30); any king who provoked a war without knowing in advance the capabilities of his army would be out of his wits (Luke 14:31-32); the good shepherd knows his sheep and knows them by name (John 10:1-16), etc. The end of the pastoral mission is not the *cognoscere* but the *ministrare*. However, one cannot serve without knowing; knowing is not enough in itself, yet it is necessary.[90] For this reason all pastoral action must be aware of the human condition so that it can achieve the greatest possible efficacy. The knowledge is provided by an auxiliary science of pastoral theology, a human and not theological science, that we shall hereafter call the pastoral propaedeutic.

The discovery of a method that without any fear could be applied to the study of a real situation with regard to an effective pastoral effort has had an extraordinary success, especially in French-speaking countries. So great has it been that religious sociology, along with the strongly universalist emphasis of Le Blas, has succeeded in establishing itself as an irreplaceable auxiliary study. In practice it is for many a pastoral propaedeutic in the sense in which we use it here. Excessive claims,

90 Cf. C. Floristán, "Pastoral: Ciencia y arte," *Lumen*, VII (1958), 314-317.

however, have been made regarding its use in the care of souls, as if pastoral actions were not effective because ecclesial actions are often carried out without taking the means into account. We must certainly take into consideration the kind of ground to be sown, as is indicated in the parable of the sower in the Gospel, but let us not go so far as to forget all about the inner fertility of the seed, nor the necessary job of disseminating it.

"Planning intelligently to bring about the advent of the Kingdom of God is certainly a pastoral method more worthy of both God and man than a day-to-day activity carried on with no long-range aims and no systematization," Groner wrote. "The shortsighted pastor is neglecting one of his spiritual duties."[91] In other words, "if theology is the science of God and man's relationship to God, it supposes man's knowledge; in order to reach the real, concrete man it is as necessary to have recourse to sociology as it is to history."[92] The mission of preaching the Gospel that Jesus gave to the Apostles was directed not to souls but to "all nations" (Matt. 28:19), "to every creature" (Mark 16:15), which means to men subject to all kinds of historical contingencies.[93] However, man is spirit incarnate and as such is influenced by all natural causes, whose free course is respected by the almighty action of divine grace. "God, who is Lord of the supernatural order, is also Lord of the natural order. He has established his laws, and psychological observation obliges us to note that, at least ordinarily he respects them."[94]

91 F. Groner, "L'office de statistique ecclésiastique pour l'Allemagne Catholique," *Lumen Vitae,* VI (1951), p. 184.

92 J. Labbens, "La sociologie religieuse en France," *Sociologie Religieuse, Sciences sociales* (Paris, 1959), p. 29.

93 Cf. W. Schöllgen, "Recht und Notwendigkeit der Pastoralsoziologie," *Anima,* XII (1957), 16-24.

94 F. Boulard, *Primeros pasos en sociología religiosa,* Sp. tr. (Vitoria, 1955), p. 91.

This sociological declaration does not apply to the religious phenomenon in its transcendental aspect but simply in its external acts, since "the work of God remains in itself mysterious and imperceptible," as G. Grasso maintains. "But its *visible effects,* and above all the work of man and the social environment, can be perceived and studied by a sociological and historical investigation, keeping in mind their possibilities and limitations."[95]

In conclusion we could say Catholicism's religious sociology can study the *Corpus Christianum* more or less profoundly but the *Corpus Christi* will remain outside its limits.[96] J. F. Motte says in summary that "it is neither the theologian nor the sociologist who runs things in the cure of souls but only the pastor to whom the flock has been entrusted. Nevertheless, to perfectly complete his job, the pastor has need of those two scientists, one of whom passes on to him the message of heaven and the other the message of earth. No matter how different these two messages may be, they cannot be kept in separate compartments. They are the two complementary expressions of the one single message of God, Lord of Heaven and earth."[97]

If we analyze the sources of Le Bras' religious sociology we see that fundamentally they boil down to these four: historical, geographical, psychological, and strictly social.[98] Le Bras says that there are three main sciences

95 G. Grasso, *Elementi di sociologia religiosa,* Turin, 1955, p. 21; cf. F. Houtart, *La sociologie religieuse, auxiliare de la pastorale* (Louvain, 1955), p. 6.

96 R. Mehl, "Dans quelle mesure le sociologie peut-elle saisir la réalité de l'Eglise," *Rev. His. Phil. Rel.,* XXXI (1951), 429.

97 J.-F. Motte, "Sociologie et pastorale," *La Maison-Dieu,* XXXVI (1953), 102.

98 G. Le Bras, *Études de Sociologie Religieuse,* Paris, II (1952), 557, 624, 705, etc. In my doctoral thesis, *La vertiente pastoral de la Sociología religiosa* (Vitoria: Editorial Eset, 1960), I analyzed the application of religious sociology to pastoral work.

that have an immediate relationship with sociology: geography, history, and psychology. If we meditate quietly on the factors which intervene in man's life, even in its religious aspect, we shall see that they can be put into the following four statements:

1. Man lives in space.
2. He lives in society.
3. His body encloses a psyche.
4. He is subject to time.

The parish also participates in all these characteristics, since it comprises a social and psychological, geographical and historical human world. Let us look at these four characteristics.

(1) *Geography*

The parish fosters a close relationship with the local scene. Without a local territory there is no parish, as we shall see later on, if we ignore so-called personal parishes, which do not come under our consideration anyway. Geographic studies were the first studies undertaken in religious sociology, applied to the parish as an elementary study unit. The next step was to make religious maps.

Each parish has its own geographic contours. The influence that physical factors have had on religious life is evident, although the fact is that none has come to exercise an overwhelming force.

The Church, the diocese, and the parish were born in the large cities, as most ideas are. Evangelization passed from the cities to the country, just as centuries later dechristianization would. The mountains, bodies of water, and forests are the natural obstacles that protect or interrupt religious currents. Religious life is better preserved in the mountains than on the plains, although at times without any great warmth of life since it is there too that customs and traditions are best perpetuated, and these are not always very vital. A rapid Christianization or dechristianization is thus in proportion to the ease of communication and travel.

If the rural parish is poor in parishioners with human qualities then an intense religious life will be difficult because of the lack of dynamic elements. But an excessive demographic concentration or broad parish boundaries will likewise be an obstacle to good parish government. There is no real parochial pastoral campaign possible if the parish is not of human proportions (4000 to 5000 members, as the sociologists point out).

Many parishes within one given region are subject to the same economic, political, and social influences. If a dechristianization movement begins within that zone one parish alone will be unable to contain it. Normally it proceeds from the city and is always to be most feared in the more conservative regions. Accordingly, pastoral activity ought to consider the zone as a unit of apostolic operation.

Once a city is well Christianized, the Christianization of the whole region over which it exercises a strong influence is assured. Urban parochial pastoral technique, nevertheless, is difficult because of the fact that the modern city has two dimensions: a geographic dimension —the location of one's home—and a functional one—a variety of distinct activities. It is because of this dual reason that the city requires a nonparochial pastoral complement much more urgently than rural areas.

The parish church ought to be in the strategic center of the parish; furthermore, the more places of worship, the more frequent the sacramental life of the faithful. But let there be no doubt: the difficulty of carrying out a common pastoral effort will grow accordingly. This common pastoral effort ought to be attempted without diminishing the number of places of worship.

(2) *History*

It is impossible to get to know human phenomena without delving into history. "The present," says Le Bras, "is the most recent chapter of history and the past, although it is also something more, is also its preface."[99] There is a general correlation between the historical tradition of a people and their character.

History, while being a fundamental science in the study of sociological problems, is also fundamental to the investigation of pastoral situations. Without history there is no true pastoral theology; likewise, without history the context of a pastoral propaedeutic is missing.

Christianity is to be found in history and history in Christianity. In fact, all of secular history should be related and connected to the history of salvation. Christ is the measure of all history. History's beginning is the creation by the Word; its summit, Jesus' Resurrection; its end, Christ's Parousia. For the Christian, history is not something cyclical that is invariably repeated nor is it anything like a continuous and uninterrupted succession of events. Christian history is event and succession; it presents continuities and discontinuities. In short, it is progression.[100] It exhibits decisive moments—*Kairoi*—in which salvation history is manifested with a special intensity. The concept of *Kairós* is thus very important for pastoral work in its propaedeutical and theological aspects. Biblically, *Kairós* is the decisive moment that God indicates in the salvific plan, whether its validity be

99 Le Bras, *op. cit.*, v. I, p. 106.
100 J. Daniélou, *El misterio de la historia*, Sp. tr. (San Sebastián, 1957), p. 13.

universal (Tit. 1:2; 1 Tim. 2:6; 1 Tim. 6:15) or specific (2 Tim. 4:6; Luke 1:20).[101]

The best introduction to the pastoral aspect of a parish is a knowledge of its history. In a general way history really explains the parish's present social composition. With the key of history in our hand we shall know a parish's present and future. Perhaps one can explain historically the religious abstention of one class, the destructive atheism of a minority, a people's lack of confidence in their priests, the weakness of families, the social immorality of some businessmen, youth's disinterest in religion, etc. We repeat: without history there is no profound pastoral work at the parish level, neither on a theological plane (Scripture and Tradition are history) nor on the human plane (sociology is the history of today).

(3) *Psychology*

It can be said that, apart from theological aspects, the psychological question is at present the dominant element in the care of souls. If in truth pastoral work is a task requiring the association of God and man, which is to say grace and virtue, then all of man's psychic components will come into play. The psychologist's subject is man as an individual and as a social being. The difficulty of such a study is evident. "The most skillful use of existing methods," said Pius XII, "does not succeed in penetrating the psychic zone, which forms the center of the personality and remains forever in mystery."[102] The human personality, which according to the Pope is "man's psychosomatic unit as determined and

101 G. Delling, "Kairós," *Th. Wört. N.T.* (Stuttgart), III, pp. 456-465.

102 Pius XII, Speech to the Third Int'l. Cong. of Applied Psychology (April 10, 1958), *Ecclesia*, XVIII, 1958.

governed by the soul,"[103] is Creation's most brilliant work. Its attitude toward God is what religious psychology tries to analyze.

Pastoral psychology is religious psychology applied to the care of souls. The parallel between psychological action and pastoral action is the same as that existing between grace and psychic tendencies. This parallelism, according to A. Godin, is twofold: in the first place intrinsic, on the level of the work of salvation in a strict sense, and also extrinsic, on the level of full manifestation of the fruits of grace.[104] In order for divine charity to install itself deeply, he affirms further on, once possessed more surely and comfortably, or to manifest itself more fully in individuals and in society, it is the human composite as such which needs to react and submit itself as much as possible to the dynamic orientations conferred on it through grace by means of free will.

The transcendence that the problem of faith is acquiring in the present-day care of souls makes the pastoral study of the human psychic situation highly important since, as Goldbrunner declares, faith resides in "man's very center, in his person. All of man's being comes to grips with Christianity. In the modern age, faith and man are situated side by side and develop one another reciprocally."[105] So it is that man's personal dimension emerges as the crossroads of humanism and Christianity, of anthropology and theology, of man and faith.[106] The psychological analysis of the individual's personal and social reactions constitutes psychology's greatest contribution to pastoral work. Without the full and mature

103 *Ibid.*, p. 441.

104 A. Godin, "Pastorale et psychologie," *Nouv. Rev. Théol.*, LXXX (1958), pp. 166, 167.

105 J. Goldbrunner, *Pastoral personal, Psicología profunda y cura de almas*, Sp. tr. (Madrid, 1956), p. 14.

106 *Ibid.*, p. 17.

participation of the human person there is no real Christianity, just as there is no faith without a *personal* reply to God's call.

Modern anthropology has advanced in two directions that cannot be overlooked from the point of view of the care of souls. One trend has succeeded in discovering the depths of the human soul and the other has made known the existential relationship between man and the world. The first direction has developed the profound relationship that exists between faith and life, starting with the personal relationship that faith demands and the human person's demand for encounter. It has been stated that "the development of oneself is the fundamental of the Christian's development."[107] The study of the relationship between man and the world has come to the conclusion that neither one can be thought of separately. This explains religious psychology's chief relationship to pastoral theology and to other studies forming the pastoral propaedeutic.

Religious psychology has a broad contact with theology, to which it is subordinate when considered as a practical study. It receives from theology its theoretical postulates and must undertake its investigations in line with theology's modifications. The apostolate requires first of all a theological contribution and next a knowledge of the man one is going to try to investigate. Herein lies the fundamental object of pastoral psychology.

The application of pastoral psychology in the parish is tremendously useful. Above all it will help in getting to know the religious mentality, that is, the profundity with which the word of God has been received. If the religious mentality is not good, this indicates that a collapse of apparent religiousness is coming sooner or later,

107 A sentence of Münckner's in Goldbrunner, *op. cit.*, p. 41.

even though religious practice might be good. In general, the religious mentality is degraded or improved before religious practice is.

In rural circles the religious mentality suffers from lack of personalism; Christianity is built there more on custom than on reflection or conscience. This does not mean that customs should not be maintained but simply that Christianity ought not to rest on them exclusively. The profound Christian, the saint, is independent of all human factors and is sensitive only to grace, practicing charity intensely wherever possible and with any and everyone. Customs generally die out through the nonconformity of an individual, ruling group, or influential class.

Religious mentality in the cities runs parallel to class mentality. It is perhaps solely in urban circles and more concretely among intellectuals that ideas govern events. The elites become dechristianized before the masses. For this reason the situation is alarming when the ruling minorities are pagan in their way of thinking even though they may still go on practicing religion. The lack of well-prepared clergy devoted to this apostolate constitutes a grave danger. The rich and influential classes are precisely the first to adopt any form of progress or novelty.

(4) *The social factor*

"After the Bible," wrote Cardinal Mercier, "the most important and most instructive subject for study that the representative of Christ on earth can have is society."[108] Since the time of primitive peoples the reli-

108 Letter from Cardinal Mercier to Cardinal Gibbons, Sept. 25, 1921, *Oeuvres pastorales*, VIII, 259; cf. mention in G. Delcuve, "Conclusions de la Conférence Internationale. Réflexions sur l'état présent de la sociologie religieuse," *Lumen Vitae*, VI (1951), 387.

gious aspect has injected itself as much in social life as has the social phase in religious life. In many religions it was even impossible to distinguish the two spheres clearly. Jesus Christ is the one who drew a line of differentiation, though not of absolute separation.

Actually, there is no true community where there is no real religion, nor real religion where there is no genuine desire for community. "Where there is a single Christian, there is no Christian," says an old adage. From the Trinity, root and model of all social order, on through the Church and the sacraments, down to the celebration of the Eucharist—all is community. There is a common life between Christ and ourselves—sanctifying grace. With Him as head we form the *communio sanctorum.*

The parish is a social body, born as such by ecclesiastical disposition and developed historically according to the religious forces of cohesion or extension. We have already examined its historical development.

The parish's current socio-ecclesial structure offers a good subject for a sociological study. By this we do not mean to say that the essence of the parish lies in this social conglomerate, but simply that the parish, like the diocese and the Church, is visible socially.

Modern sociology tends by choice to study the so-called social energy factor. It is not enough to know the social energy factor or its structures. The possibility of a religious sociology acceptable to a Catholic and its application to pastoral work is undoubtedly the result of the work of the French thinker Gabriel Le Bras, the father of present-day religious sociology.

What interests us here is the sociology of the parish. As a religious organization the parish is composed of a structure and a life. It has two profound points of reference: one is the profane society in which it lives and the other is the heavenly society toward which it tends. The study of religious society concerns itself with the clarifying of the composition and coordination of these three worlds. In other words, it studies the structure and vitality of religious society in itself and in relation to profane and inspired society, between which it lives in perpetual tension.

According to religious sociologists,[109] there are four aspects which invariably appear in the study of every religious society. They are:

1) A theoretical system. Among primitive peoples, it was myth; for modern man it is doctrine, and in Christianity it is the message of salvation sketched in the Credo. It is generally a system of truths announced by divinity. In Christianity it is the sum total of revelation.

2) Actions of cult and worship. This is man's answer to myth and revelation. It is normally a sacrifice. In Christianity it is worship or the liturgy.

3) Moral relationship of members of the community among themselves and with other men. This is the ethical, moral aspect. In Christianity it is the practice of the great commandment of charity.

4) A community structure. This is the factor which organizes religion, which distinguishes hierarchies and classes of members, which separates priests from the rest of the faithful. In Christianity it is canon law.

While the first three aspects comprise the community's religious life, the last one limits itself to manifesting the community's own kind of structure. The first

109 J. Wach, "Religionssoziologie" (Tübingen, 1959), pp. 19 ff.; G. Le Bras, "Rhythmes du monde," 27th yr., new series, I (1953), 59-61.

three indicate the relationship of pastoral work to religious sociology and the last aspect indicates the relations which this latter science has with law.

2) *Religious sociology*

(a) *Sociology of the community*

Sociologists who have studied the parish agree in saying that the sociology of the parish is a branch of the sociology of religion and that it ought to be approached from the viewpoint of the community, which is to say as a system of social relations.

The community is a universal society with a local basis.[110] Its most essential elements are:

1. The *ecological* element, that is, the community's relation with the space in which it lives. Within this element we study the principle of *vicinity* and *natural areas* which comprise the community.

2. *Structural composition* of the community, which is to say groups (whether spontaneous or organized), group leaders, classes, etc. The central problem of a group will always be its *integration,* which depends upon its structure.

3. *Typology* of the community, which presupposes certain historic, economic, and cultural facts. In this regard we ought to have an agrarian sociology, an urban sociology and a sociology of the relations between the city and the country.

(b) *Sociology of the parish community*

According to Father Fichter, ". . . demography, sociography and structure ought to be considered simply

110 Cf. R. König, *Grundformen der Gesellschaft: Die Gemeinde* (Hamburg: 1958).

as what they are: a valuable preliminary to sociology and a basis for information on which sociology can operate. But we should not confuse this preliminary study with the central object of scientific sociology: behavior types, functions, relations and life processes of the group."[111]

In order to develop a sociology of the parish one must start out from certain fundamental concepts.

The first thing to find out is whether the parish is a natural human activity and what its characteristics are, in order to later investigate the religious cohesion of the parish community. This requires that we know psycho-sociologically the community's forms and patterns of belonging.[112]

According to Houtart, it is necessary to analyze sociologically the parish institution, which comprises the following steps:

1. Sociological analysis of the functions carried out by the parish priests.

2. Psycho-sociological study of the different degrees of membership in the parish institution.

3. Sociological analysis of the parish nuclei, i.e., the persons who carry out the main functions in the parish community.

4. Sociological analysis of the functions actually performed by parishes, above all nonsacramental functions.[113]

In brief, if the object of scientific sociology is the

111 J. Fichter, *La paroisse urbaine comme groupe social* (Le Puy), 84-94.

112 Cf. H. Carrier's important study, *Psycho-Sociologie de l'appartenance religieuse* (Rome: Gregorian University, 1960).

113 F. Houtart, "Sociologie de la paroisse comme assemblée eucharistique," in *La paroisse se cherche, op. cit.*, 113-114.

study of social groups, this must also be the main object of parish sociology.

3) *Pastoral theology*

The structure of the parish as a religio-social entity is determined by the Code of Canon Law, just as its parochial life is in the final analysis a field for pastoral theology. Pastoral theology's mission is not to change canonical structures as presented in the Code, although it may make many suggestions, nor can canon law attempt a profound study of the total religious life of the parish. Trying to draw up an exhaustive concept of the parish by means of law alone is as incomplete an undertaking as overlooking parish law in an effort to obtain a complete pastoral idea of the parish. Law studies ecclesial structures from a certain angle of its own; pastoral theology determines the vital function of the actions by which the Church is built. Parish law supplies the first and most visible elements which make up the parish unit; pastoral thought on the parish offers a view of its vital functions. Law shows us the *Ecclesia iuris;* pastoral theology shows the *Ecclesia caritatis.* However, any opposition between these two aspects has been rejected by Pius XII's encyclical *Mystici Corporis Christi.*[114] Christ's Church is one, and the theological view of the parish will be one. Properly understood, the juridical and social structure of the Church is not a "lesser evil" but instead an integral part of the Lord's design. *Per visibilia ad invisibilias*—from law and sociology in the Church, the diocese, and the parish to the *salus animarum.* But if spiritualism is a grave danger for the Church, an overemphasis on juridical and sociological factors is no less dangerous.

114 *AAS,* XXXV (1943), 224.

(a) *Juridical considerations*

There is no single school of thought prevalent among present-day canonists regarding the juridical definition of the parish. For many of them, Canon 216, based on an affirmation of the Council of Trent,[115] is not an authentic legal definition.[116] This says in short that the parish is *distincta pars dioeceseos, cum peculiari ecclesia et populo determinato peculiari rectori commissa, qui tamquaen proprius eiusdem pastor curam animarum habeat* (a distinct part of the diocese, with its own church and a distinct part of the population, and its own rector as the proper pastor of that territory, put in charge of it for the care of souls) (c. 216, 1). Actually it is a clarification of terms to distinguish the *paroeciae* from *quasi-paroeciae;* on the other hand, it is not found in the *De parochis* chapter nor under the title *De beneficiis ecclesiasticis* but in the separate section *De clericis in specie.* It is actually a description of the territorial parish.

The parish is called *paroecia* in canon law, though not always with the same meaning. The Code speaks more of pastors than of parishes. Notwithstanding, let us try to examine the juridical elements that make up a parish, each one's importance and their mutual relationship.

(1) *Distincta pars dioeceseos*

We have already seen that, according to the New Testament, the Church exists totally in each of its dioceses or local churches, which in turn totally contain the entire Church by concentration, not by division. In most cases Paul means the local church when he says

115 Sess. XIV of ref., c. 9; sess. XXIV of ref., c. 13.
116 H. B. Noser, *Pfarrei und Kirchgemeinde. Studie zu ihrem rechtlichen Begriff und grundsätzlichen Verhältnis* (Fribourg, Switz., 1957), pp. 14, 15.

ekklesía.[117] That is to say, the universal Church becomes an event through the celebration of the Eucharist and is visible in the local church. Karl Rahner sums up our opinion when he says: "The Eucharist as a local event takes place only in the Church, and the Church herself becomes a total event in the fullest sense through the local celebration of the Eucharist."[118]

The parochial community adds a characteristic element, that of proximity, in virtue of which the people living in a specified territory form a natural community. The territory thus determines in a special way the local community that celebrates the Eucharist.

This *pars* is precisely the natural territory in which a determined number of persons make their homes who among themselves can form a Christian community, of such a size that it can be governed by its own pastor. Territorially, the parish forms part of the diocese.

The parish is distinguished from the diocese not only because the Eucharist is celebrated by a *full priest* (the bishop) on the diocesan level but because the parish is a local community of neighbors. In the parish the Church happens, or "occurs," through the eucharistic celebration, *per modum participationis.* The diocese, on the contrary, is a local Church that consists of one or more local eucharistic communities, each one living in a *pars,* with the natural limitations of a group of neighbors. The bishop shares his priesthood with presbyters of *secondary rank* when his local church exceeds the limits of a community of neighbors. Then the diocese is split into parts in a natural manner and as determined by law. This is what has happened historically, as we have already seen.

117 A. Wikenhauser, *Die Kirche als der mystische Leib Christi nach dem Apostel Paulus* (Münster, 1934), p. 4.
118 K. Rahner, "Primat und Episkopat," *Stimmen der Zeit,* CLXI (1957), p. 330.

The territorial principle is a fundamental one in the theology of the Church, the diocese, and the parish, as well as in the Christian cure of souls. It is not, of course, the only principle but it is the first and most natural. Without a "special Apostolic indulgence" (c. 266, 4) one cannot found any parishes other than territorial ones. For this reason the *territorium* is an integral part of the parish. Juridically, this is not necessary in view of the fact that there are parishes without territory, such as the so-called private or personal ones. As a matter of fact, jurists, although not all of them, consider territory as something accidental to the parish.[119] Since what we are striving for in this book is a pastoral meditation on the normal parish, without paying any attention to those few exceptions, let us go on the assumption that territory is essential to the real pastoral concept of the parish.

(2) *Populus determinatus*

The Code decides on the basis of domicile or quasi-domicile which of the faithful are attached to a particular parish (c. 92, 3) or pastor (c. 94, 1). It is clear that the faithful living habitually in a parish's territory are parishioners of that parish. It also seems clear, at least pastorally speaking, that a pastor has under his care not only those who have their residence or quasi-residence in his parish but also anyone living there, even if only temporarily. In times past it was easy to decide who made up the *populus determinatus*. Today, because of the demographic revolution, industrialization, and urban concentration—in other words, the by-products of modern technical advances—men move about more quickly and frequently than ever before. As a result, it is no

119 Noser, *op. cit.*, p. 26.

longer easy to determine who belongs to a particular parish, especially in the large cities. Consequently, one can speak of a *populus determinatus* with reference to the territory of a parish or with reference to its own pastor. That is, not everyone in a parish's territory at a given moment belongs to it but nevertheless all come under the pastor's *cura animarum* (c. 460, 2).

However, the Code enumerates the pastor's rights and duties with respect to *his* parishioners:[120] he himself must celebrate the divine services, administer the sacraments to the faithful, preach the faith, teach the catechism to the children, etc. But it does not order the faithful to fulfil their obligations in the parish; it says "when they can conveniently do so" (c. 467, 2), which is to say that they should participate in the services and listen to the word of God in their own parish unless this creates an inconvenience. This indicates that the parish community is not the only community in the Church within the diocese, although it is the first and fundamental one. From the Code one deduces that there are other, nonparochial Christian communities that come in contact with parishioners since these parishioners can hear the word of God in them and participate in the Eucharist, activities which constitute the essence of an ecclesial community.

The parish *populus determinatus* is an ecclesiastical right since it proceeds according to division and not *full concentration* of the local church. That is, it proceeds according to an ecclesiastical disposition clearly formulated for every local church, first by Trent and later by the Code (c. 216). The concrete determination of the territory of a diocese is also an ecclesiastical right. The fact that the universal Church is present completely in local churches, under the deaconry of a bishop, is a divine

120 CIC, c. 467:1; 1344:1; 1329-1332; 863; 892:1; 873:1.

law, as is the fact that there should exist various dioceses.

The diocesan Church is only present in the parish community when directly presided over by its bishop as *plenus parochus,* especially when he pontificates at the celebration of the Eucharist with the members of the parish.

It is evident for natural and theological reasons that the Code's parochial *populus* constitutes a community. In the first place it is a body of people originally formed by all the residents of a concrete territory, customarily called *paroecia* in official juridical language. This group of neighbors, united by the fundamental bond of their mutual human nature, will never be able to achieve their ends in a constant and sure manner unless they live a community life. On the other hand, these neighbors are either all members of the Church, active to a greater or lesser degree, or have an indelible relation to it, even though they may not know it yet or, knowing it, still do not desire it. If baptized, they are already members of the Church and as such form part of the great *communio sanctorum,* which appears within the parish's boundaries with the visible sign of the parish community. If they do not belong to the Church, their incorporation into the parish has as its starting point the parish community, which must live in a continuous state of mission, as we shall see later on. In the present Code the laity's place is very restricted, which does not mean however that their function in the Church is entirely accessory. The present movement relating to a theology of the laity and the echo it has had, not only among laymen themselves but also among the clergy, speaks for itself.

Unfortunately, the juridical concept of a passive sort of layman, which is to say the kind that only hears and receives, has through the centuries won out over the theological concept of an active sort of layman, or in other words a man consecrated by certain sacraments for specific functions. The famous decree of Gratian, *Duo sunt genera christianorum,* brought into ecclesiastical law a concept of the *laici* with a strictly mundane or secular flavor,[121] a concept which has prevailed down to our days. The law also has a concept of the parochial *populus* almost exclusively as object of the *cura animarum.* Current pastoral theology tends to point out that the parish community is not only the object but also the subject of pastoral thought. This conception naturally depends on the meaning and capacity that the layman has in the Church.

The canonists are in general agreed that the *populus* is one of the essential elements of a parish, from a canonical point of view.[122]

(3) *Peculiaris ecclesia*

The word "ecclesia" is applied by the Code to indicate the universal Church, the particular one (c. 1495, 2), and the parish place of worship. The *ecclesia paroecialis* is also frequently called *fabrica ecclesiae* or simply *fabrica.* It is the sacred building dedicated to divine worship with the purpose of permitting all faithful Christians to celebrate the memory of our Lord in the best way possible (c. 1161).

Permission for construction of the church rests with the bishop, the true liturgist of the local church. The acts of erection (c. 1162, 1) and dedication (consecration or blessing, c. 1165, 1) are canonically its funda-

121 Gratian, Dec. II, caus. XII, q.I, c.8; cf. E. Sauras, "El laicado y el poder cultural del sacerdote. ¿Existe un sacerdocio laical?" *Rev. Esp. Teol.*, XIV (1954), 275-326.
122 Noser, *op. cit.*, p. 33.

mental steps. From the moment that it is dedicated to worship through the dedication it is *ecclesia sacra.*

Juridically, the parish church is not an essential element of the parish, although it is the most visible symbol and the central point of religious life. It is the house of the parish community, the sacred building that protects the altar (tabernacle), around which the *plebs sancta* assembles to celebrate the mysteries of the Lord.

Of all the churches in a diocese, the most important is the *ecclesia cathedralis,* on whose altar the local church takes place through the eucharistic celebration of the bishop. This church is the only one which in a perpetual way has the *cathedra* of the bishop, the direct and legitimate bearer of the Word of God. In the rest of the diocesan churches the pulpit is the place where one of the bishop's collaborators proclaims the Word.

It is not a coincidence that the word "ecclesia" should be applied to the Church as well as to the parish temple. "All of God's purpose," writes Yves Congar, "consists in making humanity, created to his image, a spiritual and living temple where he not only dwells but communicates himself and receives the worship of a totally filial obedience."[123]

From Genesis to the Apocalypse, the Temple is a symbol of God's presence. First of all God is present in creation; all of Nature is therefore like a single cosmic temple. In the second place, God lives through grace in the hearts of the faithful; for this reason, according to Paul, the Christian's body is a temple of the Holy Spirit. And finally, God is essentially in Jesus Christ through the hypostatic union; Jesus is the temple of God.

Congar says that these are therefore three degrees, along the lines of St. Thomas: "general immanence of

123 Y. M.-J. Congar, *Le Mystère du Temple* (Paris, 1957), p. 7; cf. especially pp. 277-296.

God in his creation, immanence in his free and rational creature, and a singular and supreme immanence in Jesus Christ" (p. 282). Presence of God is the first form, inhabitation is the second form, and hypostasis the third. The three types of temples are thus cosmic, spiritual, and theandric.

In Jesus ". . . dwells all the fullness of the Godhead bodily" (Col. 2:9). This being so, Jesus is the eucharistic bread and the head of the community of all the faithful. "For this reason," says Congar, "our churches are also temples: they are the places which shelter the sacramental body and the mystical body of Jesus Christ, the altar (tabernacle) and the assembly of the faithful. In truth, there is no perfect temple other than the Body of Christ, but the Body of Christ is also sacramental and mystical" (p. 287-288).

Our churches, because they contain the Body of Christ eucharistically as well as mystically, and because they live in continuous incarnation in the Church, are called *ecclesiae*. They are in summary a symbol of Christ, who is the original temple of God.

(4) *Officium et beneficium paroeciale*

Thanks to the renewal of religious life under way today in all spheres of the Church, we can be said to be witnessing a critical moment in the medieval concept of the benefice.[124] In the Code this concept still exists, always united however to the office or ministry (c. 1409).

The New Testament made the Apostles' sustenance completely legitimate when, in His instructions to the Twelve, Jesus told them to take nothing at all with them

124 L. de Echeverría, "Estructura ideal del patrimonio eclesiastico," *Rev. Esp. Derecho Canon.*, V, (1950), 75.

because "the laborer deserves his living" (Matt. 10:10; Mark 10:8; cf. Deut. 25:1). Even Paul, although he declared that he himself worked, "so as not to be a burden to any" (1 Thess. 2:9) and that he worked with his own hands to provide for his companions (Acts 20:34), nevertheless maintains that it is only right that "they who minister in the temple eat what comes from the temple, and that they who serve the altar have their share with the altar" (1 Cor. 9:13), as the Lord directed. He did not avail himself of this right, however, in order to be freer in the preaching of the Gospel.

Nevertheless, the history of the parish shows us that the salary of the apostolic worker grew to such proportions by the time of the Carolingians that not only was it openly craved by the clergy and lords but at the same time it shoved into the background the office's fundamental idea of ministry or service.

Bad jurisprudence undoubtedly favored this state of affairs. This does not mean that the law itself brought it on but merely that out of a corrupt situation grew a bad law, and this bad juridical science favored the whole system. We can cite Pius XII's statement that "the discipline of Canon Law is aimed at the salvation of souls and all its regulations and laws tend principally to this that men may be made saints by grace of God and so live and die."[125] The *suprema lex* of Canon Law is thus the *salus animarum*, and yet it is very significant that this should have to be affirmed by Pius XII and repeated by so many jurists.[126]

125 Pius XII to students of the Roman College, June 24, 1939, *AAS*, XXXI (1939), 248.

126 R. Hagen, *Pfarrei und Pfarrer nach dem CIC* (Rottenburg, 1935), p. 202; Noser, *op. cit.*, pp. 32, 50.

There is no agreement among contemporary canonists as to whether the *beneficium* is of the juridical essence of the parish. Since in fact it always appears united to the *officium,* which is essential to the parish, the matter has no practical importance.

The Code calls the parish ministry "officium paroeciale." The phrase appears only a few times[127] since normally this ministry is called simply "paroecia."[128] That is, when the word "paroecia" does not stand for parish territory, it normally means "officium paroeciale."[129] The parochial ministry is definitely the parish's most essential canonical constitutive element. All the rest are related to it: the *territorium* is the geographic place where the cure of souls takes place; the *populus determinatus* is composed of the people on whom the parochial action concentrates and who develop it among themselves; the *ecclesia* is the temple where the main work of the cure of souls unfolds, which is to say the proclamation of the Lord's death through the Eucharist. For this reason it is not surprising that *ecclesia* and the parochial mission should have been so clearly identified in the past.

The parochial mission, then, is the *cura animarum* which, as we shall see later on, is nothing more than proclaiming the faith, celebrating the mysteries of the faith, and intensely practicing charity; in other words, it consists in building up the Body of Christ to the mature measure of its fullness, with everyone embracing truth and growing in charity (Eph. 4:12 ff).

(5) *Pastor proprius*

The *pastor proprius* or pastor of the parish is also

127 CIC, c. 420:1; 463:3; 2182-2184.
128 CIC, 192:3; 389:1; etc.
129 Noser, *op. cit.,* p. 51.

internally related to the *officium*, since fundamentally he is the priest immediately concerned with the ministry of a parish.[130] No one can be pastor without being a priest, nor can any priest be a pastor without being joined to a parochial ministry.

Although in c. 216, 1, the pastor seems to constitute the parish, nonetheless it can be stated, as we saw earlier, that the essence of the parish rests in the parochial office because of its stability (c. 145).

The pastor receives the parish *in titulum*, which is to say in a stable manner from the proper bishop under whose authority he exercises the cure of souls. For one thing this means he receives the parochial office for an indefinite time, and what is more it means that the ordinary pastor of all souls is the bishop (c. 334, 1). It should not be forgotten that until the Council of Trent only the bishop used the title *plenus parochus*.

According to Father Regatillo,[131] of the six elements that come under consideration in the parish's juridical aspect, the *populus* and *rector* are essential from a material standpoint, and *officium* is essential from a formal standpoint; the rest—*territorium*, *ecclesia*, and *beneficium*—are integral inasmuch as they perfect the essence of the parish. As far as Mickells is concerned, *populus*, *officium*, and the act of building up are essential.[132] Since really there is no *officium* without an act of building up, we can reduce the essential juridical elements to two, as H. B. Noser does: the *populus* and the *officium*.[133] But

130 Cf. K. Rahner's meditation, *Der Pfarrer. Eine Betrachtung* (Vienna, 1948), p. 16.
131 E. F. Regatillo, *Derecho parroquial* (Santander, 1953), p. 13.
132 A. B. Mickells, *The Constitutive Elements of Parishes* (Washington, 1950), pp. 11-12.
133 Noser, *op. cit.*, p. 61.

if we overlook those exceptional cases where a parish exists through a special apostolic indulgence (c. 216, 4) and limit ourselves to the ordinary parish, which after all is the object of our study, we can say that the *populus* is precisely *determinatus* by a territory, which also belongs within the essence of the ordinary parish.

This territorial element universalizes the parish in a sense, since there is a place within the parish community for all the people living there: children and old people, rich and poor, ignorant and learned, the sick and the healthy, the common man and the man of affairs.

In short, the *territorium* gives the parish a character which recalls that of each diocesan church in the sense that the Eucharist is celebrated locally. The *populus determinatus* constitutes the local Christian community, reduced to human size by the territory, so that the best possible parish work can be done there. The *ecclesia* is the visible image of the parish, the temple of God where the assembly's meeting with the Eucharist takes place in Christ. The *beneficium* is the material charitable projection of the people with their pastor. The *officium* is a full service of charity or love and the *pastor* or cooperator of the bishop is the person who makes possible the celebration of the Christian banquet.

Theological implications are continually cropping up in the Code. Sticking slavishly and passively to the letter of the law, without aiming for its spirit, is to betray the law. Jumping to the spirit of the law, conversely, and in the process acting in defiance of the letter and eventually of order itself is to tempt the law. Since in this book we are meditating on an ecclesial reality, even though it be of ecclesiastical origin, both elements ought to be studied. Otherwise we would come up either with a parish lacking any connection with the world or one incapable of growth and ascension.

(b) *Pastoral life*

The basic object of pastoral theology, as a science of the *cura animarum,* consists in the study of ecclesial actions—that is, the consideration of the essence of the Church as a bearer of salvation.

To F. X. Arnold's way of thinking, this central object is accounted for by the question, "What meaning and function suit the ecclesial actions of mediation—proclamation of the faith, liturgical-sacramental life, and solicitude for souls—in the overall picture of the salvific process existing between God and man?"[134] This question in turn gives rise to two others: "To what extent is salvation fundamentally linked to the mediation of the Church?" "What is the concrete participation of this action or ecclesial mediation in the whole process of salvation, and where does its own character lie?"[135]

It will not be wandering away from our meditation on the parish if we examine quickly the Church's pastoral actions, since the theology of the parish not only stems from the theology of the Church but its pastoral function originates in ecclesial pastoral work.

At the beginning we saw how the New Testament considered the three ecclesial actions, which have their roots in the Old Testament. "In veteri [testamento] novum latet," said Augustine, "in novo vetus patet."[136] Christ is the center of both Testaments: the Old one tells *what* He is and the New one tells us *who* He is.

134 F.-X. Arnold, "Grundsätzliches und Geschichtliches . . .," *op. cit.* (1950 edition), p. 13.
135 *Ibid.*, pp. 13, 14.
136 *Quaest. Heptateuch.*, 2.

The resounding affirmation that Jesus (N.T.) is Christ (O.T.) is precisely the fundamental burden of apostolic preaching, the beginning of salvation, and as such the starting point of our proclamation and our theology.[137]

All the prophetic Old Testament figures, both priestly and royal, are an image of the Messiah. In the first place the Old Testament announces the Messiah as a great prophet, to whom the Apostles and Christ Himself apply all the messianic prophecies: "For Moses said, 'The Lord your God shall raise up to you a prophet from among your brethren, as he raised up me; to him you shall hearken in all things that he shall speak to you' " (Acts 3:22 ff. and Deut. 18:15; Luke 4:18-21 and Is. 61:1). In the second place the Messiah was to be a priest: "You are a priest forever, according to the order of Melchisedech" (Ps. 109:4), which is to say the High Priest "who has passed into the heavens" (Heb. 4:14), having been "tried as we are in all things except sin" (Heb. 4:15), who "became to all who obey him the cause of eternal salvation, called by God a high priest according to the order of Melchisedech" (Heb. 5:9-10), "offered once to take away the sins of many" (Heb. 9:28). Finally, Jesus is the Messiah, which means the Anointed. In the Old Testament the Anointed is he who, as King of Israel, has received the horn of oil over his head (1 Kings 16:13; 10:1-9; 3 Kings 19:16) as a sign of coronation. The Scriptures often speak of Christ as King and Jesus Himself solemnly declared it before Pilate (John 18:37)

Basically these three offices are mediatory functions of the Covenant between Yahweh and His people (Lev. 26:12). In Jesus Christ they are functions of redemption which can be summed up in one function: mediation.

137 Cf. J. R. Geiselmann, *Jesus der Christus. Die Urform des apostolischen Kerygmas als Norm unserer Verkündigung und Theologie von Jesus Christus* (Stuttgart, 1951).

The three functions are clearly formulated in our Lord's declaration, "I am the way [as King], the truth [as Prophet] and the life [as Priest]" (John 14:6). The prophetic function prepares the other two; the priestly function serves the royal one and the royal function completes the first two. Of the three, the most important as a function of mediation is the priestly office, by which Christ died on the Cross to achieve the fruits of redemption which essentially are given us in the Mass. Christ is the way which leads to the Father—divine truth revealed and life capable of renewing itself and reviving. Jesus is "the faithful witness, the first born of the dead, and the ruler of the kings of the earth" (Apoc. 1:5); He "has become for us God-given wisdom, and justice, and sanctification, and redemption" (1 Cor. 1:30).

Jesus not only had these three powers, as can be recognized from the foregoing texts, but shortly before ascending into heaven He transmitted them to His disciples: "Go, therefore, and make disciples of all nations [prophetic mission], baptizing them in the name of the Father, and of the Son, and of the Holy Spirit [liturgical mission], teaching them to observe all that I have commanded you [charitable mission]" (Matt. 28:19-20).

The Apostles continued the Lord's salvific work by proclaiming the Good News, baptizing converts, strengthening the baptized through the laying on of hands, celebrating the remembrance of the Lord with them through the breaking of bread, and by carrying out the great ministry of charity to every creature.

"I am with you all days, even unto the consummation of the world," Christ promised upon handing over His powers. Christ continues in the Church, which is His Mystical Body. The three actions are thus strictly ecclesial actions, since they are to be found only in the Church—that is, in communion with Christ. "The Church therefore," says *Mediator Dei,* "in common with the Incarnate Word, has this purpose, this office, this duty: to teach the truth to all men, rightly to guide and to govern men, to offer a sacrifice that is pleasing and acceptable to God, and thus to reestablish between the infinite Creator and created things a marvelous union and right order. . . ."[138]

In all three actions Christ Himself is to be found: in the proclamation, since He Himself is the whole point of the Good News; in the Eucharist, since it is His sacramental body; and in the Agape, since He is the benevolence of the Father toward a sinful world. "As the Father has sent me, I also send you" (John 20:21); "as the Father has loved me, I also love you" (John 15:9). The final message of Christ's mission to His Apostles, as we can deduce from the parallelism of these two statements, is a message of love.[139] The kingdom of God is an agape; the kingdom of God is built up through loving.

The writings of the early Church Fathers clearly demonstrate that these three actions are ecclesial actions. In primitive patristics the *Mater Ecclesia* is the mediatrix of salvation; the virgin and mother Church was the favorite symbol of Christian thinkers for the first three centuries. Without the Church there is no salvation since the Church is the bearer of salvation.[140]

By means of ecclesial actions the Church's fundamental mission becomes visible; these actions all stem from the mission which the Church must carry out from Jesus' ascension until His second coming. The more christological pastoral action is, the more fruitful it will be; the closer it draws to the charitable mission Christ ordered, the more profound it will be; and finally, the

138 Pius XII, *Mediator Dei, AAS*, 39 (1947), pp. 527 ff.

139 Y. M.-J. Congar, *Esquisses du Mystère de l'Eglise* (Paris, 1933), p. 131.

140 K. Delahaye, *Erneuerung der Seelsorgsform aus der Sicht der frühen Patristik* (Freiburg im Br., 1958), pp. 87 ff.

more the Church appears in this mission as a bearer of salvation, the more real it will be. Pastoral action, therefore, is an action of the Church in virtue of the mission conferred on her by Christ through the Apostles.[141]

The mission began when the first Christian Easter ended after an intense period of fifty days, that is, after the Savior's historic resurrection. The new Spirit of Pentecost constituted the force which was to carry the mission as far as the perfect testimony, the martyrdom of those who had been sent. For this reason the context of that mission was paschal and the strength with which it was carried out was pentecostal. This mission was supposed to end with the Parousia and so it is also eschatological. Christ came with the redemption and He continues to come in the word, in the Eucharist, and in charity, and He will come at the end of time; He is the whole point of the mission which the Church performs in the world.

In this sense pastoral theology is based on a Church dogma: it is the theology of the Church under construction, the dynamic theology of the Church. Its formal object cannot be anything but the object of the true and only theology: God known through the living Christ in the Church.[142] The more the dogmatic outlook is reduced to a static field of consideration, to the field of structures, the more urgent the task of pastoral theology becomes. When the dynamics of the Church lies eclipsed in the half-shadows then pastoral theology is scanty, because this theology is not constructed on the basis of experiences, from the bottom up, but just the opposite: it is built from the top down, from revelation

141 P.-A. Liégé, Introduction to F.-X. Arnold's *Serviteurs de la foi* (Tournai, 1957), pp. XXII.

142 Cf. G. Ceriani, "Introduzione" in *Il Giorno de Signore. Settimana de Orientamento Pastorale* (Brescia, 1953), pp. 11-12.

to situation. We agree that pastoral theology is a theory and that the practical realm precedes the theoretical realm, but this theology is never antecedent to principles. Pastoral theology must seek those principles.

It is precisely because there has been such a concentration on practical pastoral aspects and advice without any serious foundation of revelation that so many pastoral attempts and teachings have failed. Some theological expositions, more or less founded on revelation, have likewise failed because they forgot the dynamics of the Church. The Fathers called the cure of souls *ars artium* and the scholastics called theology *scientia.* Without theological science there can be no pastoral theology, just as the cure of souls will not be profound if theological richness be lacking. Someone will be sure to say that in order to be a good pastor of souls it is enough to be holy. How can a priest be holy today, though, unless he has an eagerness to grasp vital theological developments? The holiness of a priest, as distinguished from that of a lay brother or an ordinary layman, demands a *known and lived* theology. The priest, who in some way or other is always a pastor, sanctifies himself by living theologically in a special way, distinct from a layman's way. Of course, he still continues to live according to the divine commands that apply to every redeemed person. But he cannot even do this unless he lives on a certain theological level, which will depend on the mission that is his to perform in the Church. The theological course closest to a good life based on obedience to God's laws is pastoral theology, which is in no way mere pedagogy or methodology.

Modern pastoral thought looks with indifference upon techniques which do not originate from a vital theological core. A really holy pastor will never be very far from the context of the salvific mission which the Church has placed in his hands in virtue of his priestly ordination. His methods may be rudimentary, as was the case with the Curé of Ars, or perhaps exclusively personal, like those of Francis de Sales, Don Bosco, etc. The one thing sure is that the Church will grow through the contributions of his pastoral action. But the Mystical Body of Christ will not grow when the pastor is lacking in substantial loyalty to his mission even though his methods be revolutionary. Pastoral theology is not a science or an art of techniques and methods; it is a science and art which draws on one wisdom alone: the wisdom of salvation.

Pastoral theology consequently embraces three profound and universal considerations: sources, the whole, and the present. First of all it looks to its sources, *ad fontes,* at the Bible as a message of salvation, upon the history of the Church as a history of salvation, and upon theology as a service to the life of faith and charity. Then it looks to the whole, the overall picture, in order not to overemphasize a single aspect or another and thus unbalance everything. And finally it looks to the present, since our contemporaries demand that salvation be mediated to them in terms appropriate to their situation.[143]

In short we see that pastoral theology is a theological science of the Church in action, of a Church building herself, of the endless incarnation in men of Jesus Christ, who is word and life. The Church is both the subject and the object of pastoral thought and activity. If the preacher, the liturgist, or the pastor builds up the Body of Christ it is because Christ is working in them through the Church. Actually, only Christ can build up His Body and only the Church can build herself.

From what has been said we can see that all the

143 H. Fries, "Anliegen der Theologie an die Seelsorge," *Lebendige Seelsorge,* IX (1958), pp. 122-126.

Church is present in the local church. Diocesan pastoral work is therefore an ecclesial pastoral work in the full sense of the word. The bishop cannot be lacking anything at all in his functions as doctor, priest, and pastor. "The bishops, under the authority of the Roman Pontiff, are the true doctors and teachers of the faithful entrusted to them," says Canon Law (c. 1326) ; they are the ones who have received the fullness of the priesthood and as such they are the only ones capable of communicating it to others. They are the real pastors of their dioceses. "Priests are priests in subordination to their pastoral duties," says Msgr. Guerry. "They partake of the apostolic responsibility of the chief pastor of the diocese."[144] Even St. Thomas expressly says: "Bishops have as their principal power charge over the sheep of their diocese, whereas pastors and archpriests only have restricted ministries that are dependent on the bishop's authority."[145]

Christ constructs the universal Church in an invisible way by means of the Holy Spirit, and in a visible and ordinary way through the apostolic college headed by the Roman pontiff. The local church, as *Mediator Dei* says, is built up "by the voice and jurisdiction of each bishop."[146] How is the parochial community built up? The parish is constructed in the local church, not the other way around. For this reason, parish pastoral work must be totally diocesan and ecclesial; however, not all Church or diocesan pastoral work takes place in the parish, since the local church is not completely present in the parish. There is, it is true, a presence of the diocese and the Church in the parish but always in a shared way, not totally, just as the presbyter's priesthood is a

144 Guerry, *L'évêque* (Paris, 1954), p. 194.
145 Q.184, a.6 ad 2; citation in Guerry, *op. cit., ibid.*
146 Reference in Guerry, *op. cit.*, p. 164.

participation or sharing in the full priesthood of the bishop.

The parish is a Christian community of an already fixed church; it is a fraction, sui generis, of the diocesan church. The Church always begins in an area with a diocese, not a parish. The diocese is not born out of a combination of several parishes; instead, parishes start to grow out of the newly born diocese made up at first of a single parish. In this sense the diocese is the "parish in its fullness" just as the bishop is the "full pastor."

The diocese is not concentrated in each one of its parishes like the universal Church is totally present in the local churches. Nor is a local church broken up into parishes the way a state or province is broken up into counties or townships. The diocese is simply shared in parochial communities the way the bishop's priesthood is shared in the presbyter's priesthood. This does not happen merely for convenience's sake but out of an intrinsic need of the diocese and the bishop which in the final analysis is founded on the local character of the celebration of the Eucharist.

Now let us apply these ecclesial actions to the parish and see how they are developed there.

(1) *Receiving and proclaiming the word*

The *cura animarum* of modern times is faced with a problem in our parishes which would have scandalized primitive patristics. Contemporary pastoral work is presented with the urgent task of converting the baptized, in contrast to earlier ages when it had to baptize the converted. The problem is complex and as such requires today, more than ever, a close collaboration between theologians and pastors. The greater part of our people are baptized, and yet a large majority of them have a weak faith that lacks the strength necessary to engage in the evangelical practice of charity. Only a part of them can be said to belong to the eucharistic community. The normal state of affairs shows an equivalence between those who believe, those who become baptized, and those who celebrate the Eucharist. We should not think that this "normal state of affairs" has passed into history now, for it still exists today in many mission countries.

As a result, pastoral theology must come to terms with some acute problems today. Shall we stop baptizing infants? Theologically and historically speaking, this would be a false solution. What we cannot do today pastorally is administer Baptism and Holy Eucharist without certain prior and specific demands. Baptism is only for the adult who believes or for the child who will believe, providing certain precautions are taken. The Eucharist is for baptized catechumens. Why is that our acts of worship have scarcely any life? Why do our parishioners lack a firm conviction of their baptismal character? Why does our preaching fail to produce a change of heart among the hearers?

"The word of God who lives and abides forever" (1 Pet. 1:23)

The service of the word, which is a service to the faith and is considered by F.-X. Arnold the most urgent task of current pastoral work, is the first ecclesial action. Christianity is in the first place a revelation of God in the Logos, and afterwards incarnation and redemption. The Word is that by which all things have been made. There is dialogue in life of the Trinity. God made all things with His Word and the Word Incarnate is Jesus Christ, the Father's envoy to a sinful world. Revelation, the transmission of the Covenant, and the preaching of the Good News have the character of Word. "The virtue of Christ's passion," says St. Thomas, "is communicated to us through faith and the sacraments, but in different ways: the union through faith is brought about by an act of the soul; the union through the sacraments, however, is proved by the use of external things."[147]

Christ lives in our hearts through faith (Eph. 3:17) and as Paul points out elsewhere the faith cannot be extended if the word is not preached (Rom. 10:14). We are therefore united to Christ's virtue through faith, once the word has been proclaimed. "Nevertheless," says St. Thomas, "the virtue which pardons sins belongs in a special manner to the passion of Christ. Therefore, men's sins are pardoned in a special way through faith in the passion, according to St. Paul's letter to the Romans (3:25): 'whom God has set forth as a propitiation by his blood through faith.' Consequently, the virtue of the sacraments, which are ordained to destroy sins, proceeds fundamentally from faith in the passion of Christ."[148] The use of external things, which is practiced in every sacramental act, is not magical but instead demands one principle: faith. The sacrament cannot exist without the word; this is true not only at the moment of celebrating it but previously, in order that human hearts be already turned toward Christ through faith in His passion.

According to these Thomistic principles there is no action of worship in Christianity unless accompanied by the word, just as the word should not be announced without leading into a liturgical celebration. The announcing of the word is necessary in order that there be faith in Christ's passion. "A faith which did not tend toward the sacraments," says Arnold, "and which did not venerate them as having been established by God, would be de-

147 III, q.62, a.6; cf. F.-X. Arnold, *Dienst am Glauben* (Freiburg im Br., 1948), pp. 11-14.
148 III, q.62, a.5.

ficient and fictitious; a sacrament which did not flow from faith would be a kind of magic. Consequently, preaching will be deficient and fictitious too unless it leads to the mysteries, to the sacraments, as would a sacrament that were not at the same time proclamation."[149] The sacraments are a proclamation of the Lord's death, *signa protestantia fidem,* besides being a means of gaining grace. Preaching is a means of gaining grace since in the final analysis it has a sacramental character. "Utriusque poculum bibe Sacramenti et Evangeli, quia in utroque Christum bibis. Bibe Christum, quia flumen est, cuius impetus laetificat civitatem Dei."[150] In Augustine's opinion, preaching is the *sacramentum verbi,* just as the *sacramenta Christi* is the liturgy. "In truth," says Semmelroth, "the word and the sacrament are linked together as the vital and essential functions of the Church."[151]

In the logical, psychological, and temporal orders, preaching precedes worship since faith, which Paul says comes through preaching (Rom. 10:12-17), is the origin of divine filiation (John 1:12), true life for the just (Rom. 1:17), "the beginning of spiritual life,"[152] "the foundation and root of all justification."[153]

In the New Testament we see the apostolic standard regarding this first ecclesial action, consisting of the preaching of the Gospel, the Kerygma, the Good News. This age was a period of evangelization.

All the first patristic period of the Church was directed toward kerygmatic preaching, toward missionary

149 F.-X. Arnold, "Wort des Heiles. Gedankes zu einer Theologie der Predigt," *Tübingen Theol. Quart.*, 137 (1957), 10.
150 Ambrose, *Enarr. in Ps. 1; PL* 14, 940.
151 O. Semmelroth, *Das geistliche Amt* (Frankfurt, 1958), p. 151.
152 II-II, q.16, a.1 ad 1.
153 Trid. sess. VI, Chap. 8, D.801.

evangelization. The primitive Kerygma was historical and salvific, christological and paschal, Church- and community-related, eschatological and Parousial, existential and vital.[154] The *magnalia Dei*, centered in the great event of the Savior's death and resurrection, were proclaimed and the community entered into the meaning of Easter as a feast of salvation and core of the divine plan of salvation.

Later on, with the creation of other feasts, the great feast of Easter faded into the shadows and became the *dies resurrectionis*. Still later, the historical account was to gain favor and the apologetics derived from the Savior's resurrection would occupy first place in people's attention. And finally, once the primitive kerygmatic tone was lost, with the paschal tone of all salvation history disfigured and its relation to the mystery of redemption forgotten, only human moral resurrection would be talked about.[155]

The first step in preaching consists of the proclamation of the "word of salvation," the *lumen vitae*, in order for the faith to blossom forth or awaken in the hearts of the listeners. Strictly speaking this takes place between God and man, but without the preacher's mediation there is no faith. The preacher is thus a mediator of the word, a servant of the "Word of Life."

First of all he is a *herald*, a specially sent messenger. Unless he be sent his preaching is not of the Church and not Christian; furthermore, he must proclaim with decision and universality. The word is for all men; it divides those who hear it; it creates community. Its success may

154 P. Hitz, *L'annonce missionaire de l'Évangile*, (Paris, 1954), pp. 110-136; Hitz, *Primat und Verkündigung*, *Paulus*, XXVI (1954), 49; V. Schurr, *La predicación viviente en el siglo XX*, Sp. tr., (Madrid), pp. 129-183.

155 B. Dreher, *Die Osterpredigt* (Freiburg im Br., 1951), p. 172.

not be visible but if it is the true word of God it will have at least invisible fruits.

Next, the preacher is a *witness* who objectively gives a transcendental testimony. If necessary he must be a total witness, that is, a martyr. Even if this is not required he must always be a truthful witness. There is no greater treason in this world than being untrue to the Lord's Pasch, God's salvation through Christ of a sinful world. Vision is as important for the preacher as is his having been sent. A cowardly herald who declines to bear witness is as terrible as an apparent witness who really has not been sent. As preacher, the pastor should be holy in order to be a witness, since without Christian witness he cannot proclaim salvation as a herald. Paul is the model of a herald and John a model witness. Actually every real Christian is a herald and a witness at one and the same time. He is a witness because he believes and is going toward the Lord, that is, he has been converted in virtue of *metanoia,* a radical change in mind and heart. He is a herald because he is confirmed. As a witness he ought to be a contemplative, a mystic; as a herald, he ought to be a man of action. In other words, the Christian ought to be a contemplative in action.[156]

"Repent and believe in the gospel" (Mark 1:15)

The first kerygmatic stage, in which the mission of the preacher is to act as mediator in order to plant or awaken faith in listeners, is connected to the problem of conversion: "the steps of a man called by God from a world without salvation to a world of salvation in

156 L. Cerfaux, "Témoins du Christ d'après le Libre des Actes," *Angelicum,* XX (1943), 166-183; A. Rétif, *Foi au Christ et mission* (Paris, 1953), pp. 26-51.

Jesus Christ."[157] "Now this is everlasting life, that they may know thee, the only true God and him whom thou hast sent, Jesus Christ" (John 17:3). Conversion demands on God's part abundant grace and, consequently, much prayer on our part. Next, an adequate presentation of the Good News, not as some kind of higher *wisdom* but rather as a saving *paradox,* along with the evangelical testimony of the community. And finally, a certain personal movement by the convert toward the faith. God is the cause behind conversion, the Church is the place where it is carried out, and the believer is the bearer of salvation. But just as a Christian community can be the framework within which a conversion is accomplished, since its life already reflects the enjoyment of the Good News, so too this community can be an impediment to conversion. It is easy to find isolated witnesses. Can Christian *communities* be found that give witness of the Church?

The second stage of catechetical pastoral work—once the Good News has been received and, through it, faith in Jesus Christ—consists in catechesis. Once Christian life is begun, catechesis gives the knowledge to make that life more profound. It is the slow introduction to the contemplation of the mysteries of God, since faith tends toward vision.[158] During this stage the initial spirit of faith and charity should grow vigorously. The food

157 P.-A. Liégé, "The first turning to God is by faith," s.a., multicopied, p. 30. "A movement of faith is required for the justification of the ungodly. . . . The movement of faith is not perfect unless it is quickened by charity; hence in the justification of the ungodly a movement of charity is infused together with the movement of faith. . . . Hence it is clear that in the justification of the ungodly an act of faith is required in order that a man may believe that God justifies man through the mystery of Christ" (I-II, q.113, a.4).

158 Ch. Moeller, "Théologie de la Parole et Oecuménisme," *Irénikon,* XXIV (1951), 313-343.

of the sacrament is added to the food of the word in this stage. "There are two tables, one on each side in the Church's treasury. One is the table of the sacred altar. . . . The other is that of divine law, which contains sacred doctrine."[159] Catechizing amounts to conveying the word of God, causing contemplation of the Christian mystery, and doing pastoral work[160]—this means that the Bible and liturgy are brought alive and lived in charity.

And finally in this third stage, joined to a totally evangelical life, there is a deeper penetration into the Bible and the liturgy in light of the ever-central truth of Easter. Priestly theological formation ought to be a model of teaching. It is for this reason that the priest's three most important books are the Bible, the missal, and the breviary; what they all amount to is Scripture, since the last two are the Bible prayed and meditated, sacramentally incarnated in the life of the Church. "The golden age of preaching," says Moeller, "is when it is joined to Scripture (prophetic function) and the liturgy (priestly function)."[161]

When one breaks with the New Testament or primitive patristics, as in much of contemporary preaching, the result is a notable impoverishment of biblical salvation history, of paschal christocentric thought, of parousial orientation and mystical fullness.[162] Our catechesis is frequently abstract when it sets forth dogma, and sentimental when it tries to edify; it falls into a certain Monophysitism when speaking of Christ and God without any precision about shades of meaning, and it falls

159 *Imitation of Christ,* bk. IV, chap. XI.
160 Cf. F. Coudreau, "Pour un catéchisme spirituel," pro manuscripto, Kamouraska (Canada), 1955.
161 Moeller, *op. cit.,* p. 343.
162 Hitz, *op. cit.,* p. 157.

into a Nestorian sentimentality when it treats the figure of the Son of Man alone. Neither our preaching nor our catechesis operates in a sufficiently biblical and liturgical atmosphere.[163]

Summing up, then, we can say that catechetical pastoral work, which has been the primordial function of the Apostles and the Church, is composed of several stages: a) evangelical, kerygmatic missionary preaching, whose object is to announce to the world the mystery of Christ; b) catechesis or *didactic* teaching in which the elements of faith and Christian life are spelled out; and c) *didascalic* instruction which embraces a higher religious teaching.[164] "The ministry of the Word," says Liégé, "consists in receiving the message of salvation first of all (this is a job for evangelization, which is the first step of catechesis) and expanding and enriching it among believers (this is catechesis in its strictest meaning)."[165]

The parish is, above everything else, a local community of catechumens; it is a community which has received the Good News, recognizing that Jesus is the Christ, and which has converted itself through a radical *metanoia.* It is therefore a community that believes in Jesus Christ, that lives the moral consequences of the Gospel, and that practices the Beatitudes. While the age of the catechumenate has passed (although not completely, as can be seen from today's renewed need for it), catechumens have never disappeared. A catechumen is not just a convert before being baptized: any baptized person is always a catechumen, since all his life will be a continuous exercise in conversion, in turning toward

163 Moeller, *op. cit.*, p. 323.
164 Hitz, *op. cit.*, pp. 7, 8.
165 P.-A. Liégé, "Pour une théologie pastorale catéchétique," *Rev. Sc. Philos. Théol.*, XXXIX (1955), 9.

Christ, in a radical *metanoia.* The Church was born with the community of catechumens, and the parish developed from this community. Thus, there is no parish in a pastoral sense if there is no community of converts, no community of believers—in a word, an evangelical community.

The parishioner who is baptized without being converted betrays Christ, just as he who is not converted after Baptism betrays Him. To celebrate the Eucharist without being converted and baptized is also betrayal: Paul calls it condemnation. Parish pastoral work must therefore be emminently evangelical; this applies to the relationship between the pastor and his parishioners and that of the parishioners among themselves. In order to proclaim the Word one must receive it; in order to proclaim it effectively one must believe in its virtue; in order to proclaim it with total strength one must live it. It does not depend essentially on the messenger's ethical life, but if in addition he is a witness his effectiveness will undoubtedly be greater. Jesus not only said "Preach the Gospel" (Mark 16:15) but also "You shall be witnesses for me" (Acts 1:8).

Everyone who *believes* is already in a position to announce the Word to others; for this reason the parish, as a community of catechumens, is the object and subject of pastoral effort. The believer has to assimilate the Word in order to live it as a witness and announce it as a herald.

The sacramental life of the Church, closely linked to the parish community, causes a gradation in the types of heralds, or messengers. A parish's first herald is not its pastor but its bishop, the only messenger who, through his close communion with the pope and episcopal college, guarantees the truth of the Word. This guarantee passes from the bishop to the pastor. Without the headship of the pope, surrounded by his colleagues the Apostles, no one can interpret the oral or written depository of faith without deviating from the proper course. For this very reason, the parish is not a local church of the word but a local evangelical Christian community. It needs a bishop to raise itself to a full ecclesial level. The Word is in the parish community, just as it is in each believer, but not all the teaching power. The Truth is there too, but not in its full guarantee.

Furthermore, only the bishop has power to send forth, because the Church is in him. For this reason it is the bishop who ordains priests from among the confirmed and confirms the baptized. Preaching is thus an ecclesial and an episcopal task. "No one may exercise the ministry of preaching unless he has received a mission from his lawful superior, either by special grant of the faculty to preach, or by receiving an office to which the function of preaching is attached according to canon law" (c. 1328). The preceding canon (1327) says that the "office of preaching the Catholic faith" appertains to the pope in the universal Church and to the bishop in the local church.

The pastor preaches because first he has the *missio* and then secondly the *licentia.* He is not basically a preacher because of having studied theology but because he is a priest; a layman may in fact know more about theology than a priest or even a bishop, but at present he is not an *offical envoy*. And yet, as we mentioned earlier, the sending itself is not enough; the pastor must be a faithful witness. He does not receive the word from the bishop but from the *depository of the faith;* what he does receive from the bishop are the *missio* and the *licentia.* The pastor's first duty is to know the depository of the faith, transformed into word in the Bible and tradition, and transformed into prayer in the official ecclesiastical books. His preaching will not be lawful without license and will not be of the Church without the element of being sent, but above all it will not even be preaching unless its point of departure is this depository of faith. We have just declared that the priest does not preach *because* he has studied theology; actually, we must also point out that without knowing theology he cannot preach either. "And my speech and my preaching were not in the persuasive words of wisdom," said Paul, "but in the demonstration of the Spirit and of power, that your faith might rest, not on the wisdom of men, but on the power of God" (1 Cor. 2:4-5).

Before being a professor of religion, the pastor is a messenger of the word, a catechist, and a "didascalic." One knows religion by saving oneself and saving others. The more a pastor is a faithful witness to the word of God and a good co-worker with the bishop, the further parish catechesis and preaching will go. What is called for, consequently, is a faithful submission of the pastor to the word and conscientious solidarity with the bishop.

"For we are God's helpers," wrote Paul, "you are God's tillage, God's building" (1 Cor. 3:9). The pastor is the mediator of the word between God and the community under the authority of the bishop. But aside from pastors, "other capable preachers" (c. 1327:2) may be employed for that office as well. A layman can receive the mission of preaching. Naturally, what a layman cannot do is proclaim the Lord's death within the context of the eucharistic celebration, because this requires the priesthood. But there is a lot of room between solemn preaching (or the definition of a dogma by the pope) and the announcement of Jesus as Messiah that a catechumen might make to an unbeliever.

The catechumen announces in a stammering way, without a specific mission and, therefore, without any objective security, but the point is he can announce, since in his heart he has already received the faith through the word.[166] His testimony can even become perfect, in martyrdom, when he receives Baptism by blood. Another who can announce is the confirmed person, since he already forms part of the Christian militia; along with the sacrament of Confirmation he has received the mission of announcing Christ by his witness. Finally, the presbyter too announces, since his *potestas sacerdotalis* carries with it the official mission of proclaiming the Word of God not only in the world but in the more intimate atmosphere of the eucharistic community.

The parish is born in a local church, where the word has already been proclaimed. In this church, only the bishop keeps the word divine, through his communion with the college of bishops headed by the pope. But the parish cannot live without the Word of God. In the first place, there may be unbelievers in the congregation who must come into the faith through preaching. In the second place, there may be catechumens in the strict sense of the word, who are preparing for Baptism by a biblical and liturgical catechesis of the Word. Thirdly, there are baptized children there who should be catechized in a way befitting their age. And, finally, the Word is a nourishing food which no Christian can do without. If the faith of our Christians is weak, it is because they are lacking the sustenance of that nourishment. Even the eucharistic meal is often not fully profitted from because the food of the Word has not preceded the food of the sacrament.

166 "Before Baptism Cornelius and others like him receive grace and virtues through their faith in Christ and their implicit or explicit desire for Baptism. But afterwards, in Baptism, they receive a greater fullness of grace and virtues" (III, q.69, a.4 ad 2).

The parish is consequently a local Christian community that receives and proclaims the Word of God.

(2) *Celebrating the Eucharist*

"You must be born again" (John 3:7)

Ecclesial action of the word begins anywhere that men have not heard that Jesus is Christ. From the proclamation of Kerygma to the eucharistic celebration, the Church community is built along a line that follows from the word to the sacrament and ends in charity.

These are different states from a theoretical, pastoral point of view, but in reality they appear together. The community is one and the same; it is human at the start, then becomes a Church and ends, beyond time, in eternity.

The parish is a local community of catechumens who prepare themselves through catechesis for transformation into a local baptismal community. "What do you ask of the Church of God?" we ask the person to be baptized, and he answers through his godparents, if he is an infant: "Faith." We ask again: "What does faith bring you?" and he replies: "Life eternal." Then, in the baptistry, after determining that he really professes the symbol of faith and that he freely wishes to be baptized, we baptize him.

Faith always precedes Baptism, even for infants, whose faith is represented by that of their parents or of the whole Church.[167] "Faith and Baptism," says Basil, "are two means of salvation interunited and inseparable. Faith finds its fullness in Baptism and Baptism is based upon faith. They have the same holy formula in common: we believe in the Father, in the Son, and in the Holy Spirit, and it is in the name of the Father, and of the Son, and of the Holy Spirit that we are baptizing. First

167 *Catec. Rom.*, II, chap. 2, q. 33.

comes the public confession of faith, which leads to salvation; afterwards comes Baptism, which seals our entrance into the Church."[168] Cyprian called Baptism "the water of faith" and Tertulian called it "the garment of faith."[169] There is salvation before Baptism, but not without Baptism, since the health and salvation of the soul is Christ, who gives Himself to us in faith with a profound sacramental reference once we have been converted.

Baptism is the entrance into the Kingdom of God. The exorcisms signify that Christian life is a combat, a fight with Satan's kingdom; the bathing is the new birth wherein we die to sin and rise again with Christ; the anointing, which will be completed with Confirmation, amounts to entering into the royal community governed by the *Kyrios;* the white clothing is the wedding dress and the lighted candle is the new Christian light which ought to shine in the world. In truth, the Gospels refer to Baptism as a new birth and the Fathers saw it as a new creation. "Since the birth of Jesus from the womb of Mary is the beginning of salvific fullness for the world, as patristics points out, so too each man's baptismal birth in the womb of the Church is the beginning of his complete salvation."[170]

Every catechumen is born again through Baptism in the parish community. The parish church is simply a temple with baptismal font. We Christians have all received the beginnings of salvation there; we have all been parishioners at some time. The Word of God, as the food of faith, can continually be received in any Christian community; Baptism is received once. This also

168 *De Spiritu Sancto*, I, 17; *PG* 32, 117; cf. P.-A. Liégé: "Das Katekumenat im Aufbau der Kirche" in *Verkündigung und Glaube*. Festgabe für F.-X. Arnold (Freiburg im Br., 1958), p. 259.
169 Cf. mention in K. Delahaye, *Erneuerung . . ., op. cit.*, p. 185.
170 *Ibid.*, p. 170.

supposes catechesis to be fundamentally a parochial task (c. 1339) ; therefore, even though it be received outside of the parish the pastor is the one who baptizes and who remains responsible for the baptized.

The parish, a local community of people baptized in the same font, has to live decisively the consequences of Baptism both individually and collectively. This means it must be a community of believers, of converts, and catechists; in addition, it therefore must be a community of saints and must overflow with charity. Since it is formed by converts full of charity, its members ought to live through Christ, with Christ, and in Christ. They must be in the world without being of the world; they must be a Church. There is no local community of the baptized without these three features: faith in the mystery of Christ, *metanoia,* or radical change in the moral life properly speaking, and finally apostolic "warfare" for the Church.[171] The Gospel of John is witness to Baptism as a first step toward a life of salvation (John 3:5) and Paul testified to the communitarian nature of Baptism (1 Cor. 1-2).

Baptism then, is the sacrament of the first conversion. Baptism and conversion are inseparable. The ecclesial means is the parish. But the Church, we have said, is essentially eucharistic; for this reason we can see the need for eucharistic communities. Without conversion to the Gospel there can be no Baptism and without Baptism there is no Eucharist.[172] Hence the need for the Eucharist in baptizing and converting, and the need for conversion and Baptism in celebrating the Eucharist. Parochial activity not based on a balanced combination of these factors runs the risk of not being Christian,

171 P.-A. Liégé, *Das Katekumenat . . .*, *op. cit.*, pp. 257-258.
172 P.-A. Liégé, "Evangelisation" in "Catholicisme," *Encyclopédie Jacquement,* IV, col. 756.

in which case there is no inner parish, no mystical parish. There may be certain visible elements to soothe and quiet superficial anxieties but the Church as the Mystical Body of Christ is not really planted in such a situation.

Between Baptism and the Eucharist lies Confirmation, which forms with them the triumvirate of sacramental initiation into Christian life. In Baptism the pastor comes out to meet the catechumen and in Confirmation the bishop meets the baptized; in the Eucharist, it is our Lord who receives the confirmed person. The parish, the diocese, and the Church are as inseparable as Baptism, Confirmation, and the Holy Eucharist.

Through Confirmation our incorporation into the People of God and the real priesthood of the faithful is brought about, under the seal of the spirit received in full Christian maturity. One cannot understand Confirmation without a reference to Baptism and the Eucharist. The baptized party's personal holiness ought to be witnessed in Confirmation, since the confirmed person is a witness, a messenger from the Church to the world. In relation to the static character of Baptism, Confirmation is dynamic. The inner aim of the confirmed man is to come to participate fully in the Body of Christ; his outer aim is to bear witness with a mature Christian life that began with Baptism.

Because he has received the Holy Spirit, the confirmed man is a prophet; that is, he is a man of God moved by His Spirit for the building-up of the New Covenant. In addition, he is consecrated by the anointment to participate actively in the celebration of the Christian mysteries. And lastly, he is an apostle of Christ in the world since, by living sacramentally, he bears witness to the word received.

Confirmation is each Christian's Pentecost just as Pentecost is the Church's Confirmation. In the same way that the Church's Pentecost in the liturgical year ends in the Parousia, so too the Confirmation of the baptized, the personal Pentecost, has an eschatological stamp. Pentecost begins when Easter ends or, better, it is the Pasch of Christ continued in the Holy Spirit. The Christian's Confirmation is his Baptism continued in the same spirit: it is a Baptism of Spirit. Before Easter, came Christ's Gospel which culminated in the Savior's death, burial and resurrection—in other words, with the Christian Kerygma. Before the Christian's Baptism, which is his Pasch, came his evangelical life which transformed the old man, who died and rose again in Christ through grace. Without the Gospel there is no Easter and without Easter there is no Pentecost; without conversion there is no Baptism and without Baptism there is no Confirmation.

Only the bishop administers Confirmation just as only he administers Holy Orders. He is not only the first priest, the full priest of his local church, but he is also the first anointed one, the fully confirmed man. Confirmation, like Holy Orders, is a diocesan sacrament. The bishop is the ordinary minister of Confirmation and of the priesthood. Only he on whom the local church rests can ordinarily name his collaborators. In reality he ordains because he himself is not physically able to celebrate the Eucharist with all the members of his flock, because his church is divided into parishes; it is for this reason that he shares his priesthood. Herein lies the close relationship between priestly orders and the parish, since without priests there are no parishes and without parishes today there can be no fullness of diocesan ecclesial life.

The bishop confirms because the Church cannot live without witnesses. Moreover, the Church is a community of witnesses because it is a continued Pentecost. If the

Church were reduced to the priestly class alone there would be lacking in the eucharistic celebration the *plebs sancta,* the *familia Dei.* There would therefore be no worship. Jungmann tells us that "Christ is the Head and the Priest of the worship which the community celebrates; the worship becomes visible through the Church [community] under the direction of the delegated *minister.*"[173] In order that there be the Eucharist it is necessary that there be confirmed Christians.

The bishop ordinarily confirms in each one of his parishes. Because it is a local community of people baptized in the same baptismal font, the parish is the ideal place for the sacrament of Confirmation. The pastor may also confirm in extreme cases; it should be noted that no other priest, not even the coadjutor, can do so. Only the pastor becomes an actualization of the bishop in the case of danger of death for a baptized person.

Priestly ordination ordinarily takes place in the parish's mother-church, the cathedral; it is the ideal place. The bishop can also ordain in a parish church, turning it into a sort of *ipso facto* cathedral, since in the eucharistic celebration of the bishop, during which the ordination takes place, the diocesan church becomes present. It is precisely in the ordination of priests that the bishop's presbyterium becomes visible, a presbyterium from which no pastor should be missing.

We can therefore see that the parish is a local community of confirmed persons under the direction or service of a presbyter called a pastor. Confirmation and Holy Orders are like two sacramental seals of the Spirit, originally diocesan and with a close link to the parish. "The social encounter between the community of the con-

173 J. A. Jungmann, "Christus. Gemeinde. Priester," in *Wesentliche Seelsorge* (10th ed. Lucerne: von Hornstein, 1945), pp. 85-97.

firmed and the priestly mystery," says Semmelroth, "is like a sacrament of the spiritual encounter between God and men."[174]

Penance, the sacrament of the second conversion, is not strictly parochial, precisely because it can be repeated whenever the first conversion is in crisis. The weaker the testimonial life of the confirmed person, the more often confession will be necessary, and the less deeply rooted the faith he professed in Baptism, along with his Christian promises, the weaker this pentecostal life will be. Similarly, the less this faith partakes of the word of salvation—the Gospel—the less deeply rooted it will be.

In order to celebrate the Eucharist, sharing its fruits in communion, it is necessary to be converted, which means being in the state of Christian grace. In turn, the authentic celebration of the Eucharist will be the *sacrum convivium,* the *coena magna* which will keep us in a continuous state of conversion. Trying to stay away from sin is impossible without *coena magna,* without Christian testimony, without a radical renunciation of Satan, without an active faith in Jesus Christ, and without the *Verbum vitae.*

This does not mean that one should go to confession only when it is absolutely necessary. Confession is needed because it is a second conversion and in this life even the holiest of men are never completely free from sin. Confession is a return from faraway lands to our Father's house, where He is waiting for us with the banquet of life. It is a bath of life in the Redeemer's death; it is the reconstruction of our temple, and it is the Lent of Easter. Confession is a reconciliation with the Church because it is a conversion to Christ. In this

174 O. Semmelroth, *Das geistliche Amt. Theologische Sinndeutung* (Frankfurt, 1958), p. 70.

sense the ideal confessor is the bishop and, after him, the pastor.

The third sacrament of conversion is Extreme Unction, which is now to be more accurately called the Sacrament of the Sick. In biblical texts and rites we do not speak of death but instead of a return to health. "Is any one among you sick? Let him bring in the presbyters of the Church, and let them pray over him, anointing him with oil in the name of the Lord. And the prayer of faith will save the sick man, and the Lord will raise him up, and if he be in sins, they shall be forgiven him" (Jas. 5:14-15). Christ Himself sent His Apostles "to preach the Kingdom of God, and to heal the sick" (Luke 9:2). Regardless of whether or not healing of the body follows, the Sacrament of the Sick forgives sins and strengthens the soul in its final moments of combat. For the last time the Christian is anointed with the oil intended for the athletes of Christ. It is precisely when this great test presents itself that a fainting and weakening may take place, just before taking the last step of life or, better, the first one.

It is natural that the pastor be the one who normally anoints the sick of the parish. If this is physically impossible, then it ought to be the bishop, since they are his confirmed and he is the great anointed one of the diocese. The members of the local church are never alone and much less so when death approaches. Just as the first sacrament is a community one, so too is the last one. Through the parish's baptismal font we enter the Church; through the pastor's anointing, if we do not remain in that same community, we do, on the other hand, gain a place in the heavenly parish, "the Church of the firstborn who are enrolled in the heavens" (Heb. 12:23).

The sacrament of love, the sacrament that establishes a family, is strictly parochial. Matrimony, which continues what God began with creation, is a living parable of God's love for humanity and of the union of Christ and the Church. Husbands and wives engender natural life and the Church engenders supernatural life; for this reason marriage is a great mystery, comparable to that of the Church, because the Church and the marriage partners are the source of life. To control births selfishly is not only to go against the natural expansion of life according to the creation of Genesis, but is also to go against the people of the New Covenant. If Baptism makes the Church grow, marriage makes Baptism possible. Without births there is no Baptism and without Baptism there is no Church. Because Baptism is parochial, marriage is also parochial; the parish grows organically through celebrating marriages and interiorly through baptizing.

And lastly, the parish ministers to those in agony and gives Christian burial to those who have run their race and fought their last battle. All of the death liturgy, which is carried out entirely within the parish, forms a single unit whose zenith is the passage of the Christian from one life to another. This is how the earthly Jerusalem entrusts one of its members to the heavenly Jerusalem. On one side is the pastor praying with his congregation, commending the soul of the departed, while above in heaven is the holy city of Jerusalem convoked by the litanies, waiting to receive the soul of the new citizen of paradise.

Anointed and with his sins confessed—that is, converted for the last time—the dying person receives the *viaticum* from the pastor. Communion in the form of *viaticum* is his provision for the road, the last supper of the Christian who is already on his way and will not return because he has started on the road to his Father's house. The Christian's death is in reality his second

Baptism, just as Baptism is his first death. Since Christ's rising from the dead and because He did arise, the Christian's death is a wait for resurrection. To finish the battle is to rest and live a Sunday that lasts all eternity. The angels go out to meet the soul already bathed in perpetual light and lead him to the Garden of Paradise, the place of wisdom and delight; the witnesses carry him to the holy city of Jerusalem, and poor Lazarus accompanies him to the source of eternal rest.

"Do this in remembrance of me" (1 Cor. 11:24)

The Holy Eucharist, the sacrament of sacraments, is the fundamental principle of pastoral work. From Eucharist to Eucharist, from altar to altar: this is the pastoral cycle. *Introibo ad altare Dei* we say at the start of Mass; *ex hac altaris participatione*, we pray after the consecration. The consecration, the proclamation of the Lord's death, His remembrance, the memory of His Testament, i.e., the Mass: this is the center of all pastoral action. "The august Sacrifice of the Altar is the foremost instrument of divine worship; it must therefore be the head and, as it were, the center of the Christian religion."[175] The means for recognizing whether a pastoral movement has any depth is given us by the altar: it should begin and end there. This is the ascending and descending pastoral movement. "May this incense, blessed by you, ascend to you, Lord; and may your mercy descend upon us."

Christ is the High Priest, the Pontiff of the New Alliance, the only Priest. All other priests share in His priesthood. The sacrifice which Christ offered the Father once and for all was His very life from incarnation to the cross. At the Last Supper He perpetuated this sacrifice, called the Eucharist, which the Church, the Body

175 *Mediator Dei, AAS*, XXXIX (1947), 592.

of Christ, celebrates every day. The Eucharist, which means thanksgiving, is a sacrament carried out through the Mass. From the Jewish Passover Christ went on to the Last Supper, where He instituted the Holy Eucharist, the sacrament of the Christian Passover and Sacrifice of the Cross. This sacrifice takes the form of a banquet so that all Christians can take part in it. And although it was unique with Christ, its representation is preserved in the Church for the remission of sins.

The Mass is thus the sacrifice of the Church which bloodlessly but fully represents Jesus' sacrifice on the cross. Essentially, the Church is the People of God celebrating the Christian sacrifice, the Holy Eucharist. As we said earlier, without the Eucharist there is no Church and vice versa. The ecclesial community must thus be a completely eucharistic community.

The parish is the local community which celebrates the Eucharist. The pastor presides over the celebration with the complete power, received from the bishop, to consecrate the Body and Blood of Christ. But he has received not only the power but the permission as well. The pastor's power over the Eucharist is identical to that of the bishop but its use is regulated by the ordinary of the diocese. Here is still another difference between the diocese and the parish. The pastor is a priest who celebrates the Eucharist with a power inherent in his priesthood but with a permission that continuously depends on the bishop. The Church is substantially present in the parochial eucharistic celebration but not in all its manifestations. It is substantially and fully present as a local church at the pontifical Mass when the bishop is surrounded by his *presbyterium*. The pontifical liturgy is so rich and solemn because of the fact that the local church resides in the bishop, especially when he celebrates the Eucharist.

It is precisely because of the fact that not all the confirmed persons of a diocese can attend a pontifical Mass that parishes exist. In this respect all parish Masses maintain a clear relationship to that of the bishop. They will not even all be vital unless the pontifical Mass is too. The pastor is a liturgist under the authority of the pontiff of the local church. He gathers together for the celebration of the Eucharist those confirmed by the bishop, as though he were an extension of the episcopal hand. All the parishioners of a diocese celebrate one and the same Body and one and the same Blood; all partake of the same food and the same drink; it is the same Spirit that fills their hearts. "For he who eats and drinks unworthily without distinguishing the body," says Paul, "eats and drinks judgment to himself" (1 Cor. 11:29). The person who, although baptized, does not make of his life a continuous *metanoia*, a constant conversion of heart, soul, and will, does not distinguish Christ's Body. Hence the eucharistic community takes for granted the baptismal community, and in turn the community of catechumens.

Now we see once again that the parish is not the only eucharistic community just as it is not the only community of the Word. The Word and the Holy Eucharist are two necessary sources of nourishment for every Christian throughout his life. Both are best available in the Mass. "The Mass is a whole in which the proclamation of the word forms an integral part of the mystery; in order to best nourish our souls at the eucharistic table, it is an excellent idea to begin by nourishing our faith at the table of the Word."[176] For this reason the Mass is not a eucharistic sacrifice exclusive with the parish. But "where it can conveniently be done" (c. 467:2),

176 *Directoire pour la pastorale de la Messe à l'usage des diocèses de France* (Paris, 1956), No. 69.

parishioners ought to take part in the services and listen to the Word of God in their own parishes. The first contact of children with the Body of Christ, as well as with catechesis, has to be parochial (c. 1331).

"Be assiduous in prayer" (Col. 4:2)

From the moment that the Eucharist is celebrated there, the parish is the first and most natural local Christian community. Its territory localizes the parish juridically and theologically in a completely pastoral manner. Territory is therefore a spatial coordinator of prime importance for the parish. But the parish also has a great temporal coordinator: Sunday, the day of the Lord's resurrection.

In the same way that Easter is the Sunday of the liturgical year, so too Sunday is a weekly Easter. Easter is the great *kairós* of the whole liturgical cycle and Sunday is the *kairós* of the week. The eucharistic celebration of the great Easter Vigil is, as it were, the zenith of the year's pastoral program, while the Sunday parish Mass is the high point of the pastoral effort of that week. The whole year's pastoral action has to lead to or start with the *triduum Paschale* and the pastoral activity for any week must begin with or lead into the *pro populo* Mass. Only then will the parish be Christian, because its head, its cornerstone, will be Christ. From Sunday to Sunday the cycle unfolds, following the liturgical itinerary from Advent to Easter and back again from Easter at the end of Pentecost. The parish community begins its life in a state of expectancy, waiting for the Messiah, turning away from its wickedness and toward the Savior. It celebrates Easter joyously, with its members dressed up for the occasion, telling one another and indeed all the world: "Christ is risen!" Its annual apostolic mission ends with Pentecost. In the same way that the earth revolves around the sun, the parish (which is a small satellite of the diocese) moves around Christ along with the whole local church. The center of the solar system is thus Christ: the Christ who comes, the Christ who has come, and the Christ who will come. He is the Christ of today, tomorrow, and forever. The parish dresses in purple before Christmas and Easter, the two great poles of the liturgical year, because she wants to be converted to the Gospel that the Lord preached. She celebrates the Savior's birth and resurrection dressed in white as if for a wedding feast, and wears green during the time after Epiphany (manifestation of the Word Incarnate) and after Pentecost (manifestation of the Holy Spirit), because conversion to the Gospel and celebration of the sacramental mysteries are inconceivable without a deep and continuous exercise of hope in love.

"The worship which the Catholic Church pays to the Eternal and which rests mainly on the Eucharistic Sacrifice and use of the sacraments," says *Mediator Dei*, "is ordered and distributed in such a way that through the divine office it embraces the hours of the day, the weeks and the whole course of the year, as well as taking in all time and the diverse conditions of human life."[177]

The divine office—divine praise, *laus perennis*, the holy *opus Dei*—is spoken of in *Mediator Dei* as: "the prayer of the Mystical Body of Jesus Christ which, in the name and for the benefit of all Christians, is offered up to God by the priests and other ministers of the Church and by religious, devoted to this purpose by instructions of the Church herself."[178] Along with the Mass and the sacraments the divine praise constitutes the third pillar of Christian worship.

The Church's prayer is a public and official praise.

177 *Mediator Dei, AAS*, XXXIX (1947), 573.
178 *Ibid.*

Each local church offers it up solemnly in the cathedral, the parochial mother-church, through the members of the chapter, who are the representatives of the body of the diocese because they make up the bishop's senate. Secondly, it is offered up by those who have received Holy Orders. And finally, it is offered up in a solemn way in convents and monasteries. Above all presides the bishop, the leader of all diocesan prayer.

Much the same thing is true of official prayer as of preaching. We have said that in order to preach it is necessary to add vision to the sending forth, and witness to the mission. In order to pray publicly and officially with the Church it is necessary to combine devout and fervent piety with the Church's delegation. The person who prays officially but not inwardly is as pharisaical as the preacher who does not bear witness. An entire diocese's prayer life does not depend only on that of each and every one of its parishes, but rather, in a very special way, it depends on the prayer life lived in the diocesan mother-church.

The Church is a community in prayer, a community which lifts up its heart to God in order to unite itself to Him. To pray well it is necessary to be in communion with God, since prayer is dialogue with Him, speaking and listening to Him. But we cannot talk to God in prayer if our lives are not marked by a great charity. The model of all prayers is the Our Father; anyone who does not carry out what the Sunday prayer affirms does not pray well. Christian prayer requires a real desire to live a holy life and in order to live a holy life it is necessary to pray profoundly.

There is thus a complete correlation between prayer and conversion. "Not everyone who says to me 'Lord, Lord,' shall enter the kingdom of heaven; but he who does the will of my Father in heaven" (Matt. 7:21).

The most radical kind of conversion to Jesus Christ ought to precede the celebration of the Eucharist, which is the greatest of all thanksgivings and the best possible prayer. A complete series of purifications precedes the Canon, which ends exactly with the Lord's Prayer. The main task of Christian life is to be converted in order to pray better, and to pray to carry out the work of conversion.

The parish is the Church's most natural means of carrying out conversion; it should therefore be the first and most natural place for prayer. One receives the first and last sacraments of conversion in the parish, and it is there that every confirmed person ought to say his first and last prayer. From the prayer said for the child who dies to sin through parish Baptism, right up to the last prayer of the man who is baptized by death in the heavenly community, all should be interwoven with a parochial *laus perennis.* From Baptism to the grave, the Church's prayer unfolds for the Christian in a parish environment.

The Church's public prayer from Advent to Pentecost, passing through Easter, and from Baptism to the liturgy of the dead, by way of the Holy Eucharist, is the model for all private prayer. Piety must be personal; it should also be liturgical and private, communal and individual, sacramental and subjective. Just as subjective piety would be sterile and weak without the Sacrifice of the Altar and the sacraments, as Cardinal Cicognani said, so too participation in the Sacrifice of the Altar would languish without the meditation and ordinary exercises of Christian ascesis.[179]

Prayer puts man in contact with God. Christianity, however, has the stamp of incarnation, since the Word

179 Cardinal Cicognani, "Pio XII y la renovación de la liturgia pastoral" in *Pio XII y la liturgia pastoral* (Toledo, 1957), p. 37.

became man and no one reaches the Father except through the Son. The Church continues to exhibit this mark of incarnation since she is the uninterrupted incarnation of Christ. All contact between God and man has to be christological and ecclesial. For this reason we can say that the Incarnation is the law not only of preaching, worship, and the apostolate but also of prayer. The grace that prayer brings, even in the case of personal piety, is not only inner and subjective but, as Karl Rahner states, it also is always "subjective and ecclesial, inward and incarnate, existential and collective."[180] Its scale of possibilities is extremely broad, ranging all the way from the eucharistic act to a humble catechumen's devout pronunciation of the Lord's name.

In liturgical piety, which is to say the prayer which the Church offers up to the Father, the God-man encounter is always effective since grace becomes incarnate in the Mystical Body of Christ in virtue of the sacramental *opus operatum;* it will also become incarnate in the members of the Church, the baptized, if they are properly disposed in virtue of the *opus operantis.* In individual piety, however, although the grace is the same, it may happen that it does not become incarnate because the disposition is lacking. In order to pray well, it is necessary on the one hand to have the proper disposition and on the other, to include oneself completely in the midst of the people of God when as a Church they lift up their prayer to the Father. The Church's official prayer, aside from being necessary for its own subsistence and that of each of its members, only develops in a few determined *Kairoi;* they are the key moments of the prayer. All the rest of the time is devoted to the personal or individual area, but it ought to be closely

180 K. Rahner, "Personale und Sakramentale Frömmigkeit," in *Schriften zur Theologie* (3rd ed.; Einsiedeln, 1958), II, p. 134.

related and subordinate to the strictly official moments. If this subjective prayer is lacking in its appropriate place it will be difficult to achieve the proper disposition for the official liturgical prayer. But if one does not take part in official ecclesial worship, individual prayer will be impossible.

The consequences of these principles for the parish are incalculable. We have said that the parish is a local community in prayer. Put in better terms, it will be such if the piety that the local community offers up to the Father is true *ecclesial* piety. This will be true if its peak moments of official prayer are backed up by a combination of the efficacy of the Church and the disposition of all the faithful. Herein lies the first difficulty of parish spiritual life: its members are not always *disposed* to participate in liturgical worship. The great parish task is to bring about the disposition of the parishioners for the celebration of the Christian mysteries and at the same time the disposition of the pastor himself. If the Church is eucharistic and if the parish is a local eucharistic community, the first *Kairós* of a parish will take place on Sunday, the Lord's Day, at the hour of the parish Mass. Everything else is secondary and subordinate. Achieving the proper disposition of the parishioners toward that great action is a task of the greatest urgency and necessity. After the Mass, ecclesial prayer takes place in the celebration (not administration) of the sacraments; in addition to the effort to dispose Christians to take an active part in the parochial Mass, mention should be made of sacramental catechesis, typically parochial since the parish is a radically sacramental community.

A third aspect of parish prayer consists of the liturgical prayer known as the *laus perennis*. The deficiency of this prayer in parishes is frankly scandalous. For one thing, no visible example of the cathedral chapter, not even an echo, ever reaches the parish, assuming that there is a conscientious chapter to offer its praise up to the Father as representative of the diocesan community's praise. The chapter continues to have even today a great responsibility in the carrying out of the parochial *laus perennis,* since it should be the group to inspire a genuine renewal in community prayer according to the mind of the Church, in order to "strengthen hearts, blameless in holiness before God our Father, at the coming of our Lord Jesus Christ, with all his saints" (1 Thess. 3:13).

However, the type of parochial piety to be found in the evening services popularly called triduums, septenaries, novenas, etc., not only is frequently a long way from the spirit of liturgical prayer but furthermore it does not lead to official prayer. Its substance is not biblical and its development is not based on liturgical law. Evening parish services should be a liturgy of the word according to the traditional order: readings from the Bible, singing, and prayer, which includes prayer by the people as well as prayer by the celebrant.[181] These three elements symbolize the word of God as a message of the Lord, with our song as a reply, and prayer as the high point of the encounter. This order is not only traditional, in the sense that it is found in all Christian liturgies, but it likewise corresponds to the very order of salvation: revelation, the hope of humanity, and redemption. This is applied to the eucharistic celebration, to the sacraments, and to the divine office. Why are our popular parish prayer services an exception? The perfect formula would include the Bible as sum and substance, the liturgy as inspiration and the means to free us from monotony and draw us closer to the Savior, and the liturgical year as a temporary Christian itinerary.

181 J. A. Jungmann, *Des lois de la célébration liturgique,* French tr. (Paris, 1956), pp. 102-103.

Despite everything God totally respects man's liberty; within certain limits He also respects individual prayer. The Church can only think as God thinks and there is room for a great deal of liberty in each of her member's prayers. What is more, this is completely necessary.

The norm or criterion which maintains individual prayer within Church limits is the official divine praise. In this way the three dangers inherent in popular piety will be avoided: individualism, superficiality, and utilitarianism.[182] The pastor has a direct responsibility in parish spiritual life. Although the bishop is the guardian of prayer in the diocese, the immediate supervisor of the parish community is its pastor. Naturally, this does not mean that each pastor ought to invent his own parish's divine praise, just as every bishop cannot plan the official *laus perennis*. But just as in Rome appear the so-called "typical" liturgical editions for all the local churches, so too each diocese or natural diocesan group should propose the popular religious prayer for all its parishes.

Once converted and confirmed, and with a great spirit of prayer, the member of a parish community builds up the Church of Christ by celebrating the Eucharist on the Lord's Day. Precisely because of the fact that the parish is a local eucharistic community, it is also a praying community which lifts up its prayer to "the Father of mercies and the God of all comforts" (2 Cor. 1:3).

(3) *Dynamic with love*

"Practice the truth in love, and so grow up in all things" (Eph. 4:15)

We have already seen that the New Testament sup-

182 G. M. Brassó, *Liturgia y Espiritualidad* (Montserrat, 1956), p. 6.

plies the essential elements of the three ecclesial actions through which the Church is built up: proclamation of the Word, celebration of the worship of the New Alliance, and pastoral solicitude in charity. The three actions are there called *diakonía,* which is to say, service or ministry, since all three are ecclesial actions of mediation. Christ is the health or salvation of the Father sent to a sinful world, in the Holy Spirit, through the *Mater Ecclesia.* Christ comes through the Church just as the Church came through Christ; the Church is the Mystical Body of Christ. Christ is the Logos incarnate, the Paschal Lamb, the Agape of the Father and Holy Spirit. As a consequence the Church is also the Word, Sacrifice, and Love; thus she builds with proclamation, worship, and charity, serving and mediating, since the three Christian actions are gifts of the Father to His children journeying toward the Promised Land. Following the instructions of Christ, the Apostles preached the Gospel to those who did not believe, introduced converts to sacramental life, and with them formed "one heart and one soul" (Acts 4:32).

This same pastoral order was transmitted to the Church of the patristic era. The proclamation of the faith, and the sacraments of the faith, were for the Fathers the source of all Christian moral life, while the *Mater Ecclesia* acted as mediatrix of salvation through those three ecclesial actions.

According to the present baptismal rite, which in its essence and fundamental structure has come down to us from the apostolic Church, the believer who becomes baptized must keep the great commandment of love in order to achieve eternal life: "Thou shalt love the Lord thy God with thy whole heart, and with thy whole soul, and with thy whole mind, and thy neighbor as thyself" (Matt. 22:37-39). Here we also see clearly the relationship existing between faith, which comes through the word, sacrament and charity.

The same can be said about the traditional catechesis that originated with the Fathers, was preserved in the writings of the great scholastics, was reiterated in the catechism of Trent and has reappeared in recent Catholic catechisms. The division of the catechism in three parts —symbol of faith, sacraments, and commandments, in that order—is in line with the Church's pastoral tradition.

Charitable pastoral activity or pastoral solicitude, then, constitutes the third of the three ecclesial actions. According to Liégé, it "is action in the complete exercise of charity, the Lord's one greatest commandment, which it is the Church's mission to develop in the unity of its communities and bring to life through its pastoral solicitude. Briefly, this action is an aspect of evangelical morality insofar as it is an organization of government in the life of the Body of Christ."[183] The *verbum fidei* as well as the *sacramenta fidei* are expressions of agape, of charity. "If I should speak with the tongues of men and of angels," said Paul, "but do not have charity, I have become as sounding brass or a tinkling cymbal. And if I have prophecy and know all mysteries and all knowledge, and if I have all faith so as to remove mountains, yet do not have charity, I am nothing. And if I distribute all my goods to feed the poor, and if I deliver my body to be burned, yet do not have charity, it profits me nothing" (1 Cor. 13:1-3). Augustine, commenting on the First Epistle of John, wrote: "Only love differentiates the children of men from the children of the devil. Even though all of them bless themselves with the sign of the Christian cross; even though all respond 'Amen'

183 P.-A. Liégé, Introduction in F.-X. Arnold, *Serviteurs de la foi* (Tournai, 1957), p. 20.

or sing the 'Alleluia'; or go to church or build the walls of the basilicas—the children of God differ from the children of the devil only through love."[184]

Charity is the central idea of the New Testament, or rather of the whole Bible; it is the motive that inspires all the saints. Scripture sings of the marriage of God to His people, of Christ and the Church. It is a tragic but glorious love story that goes from Genesis to the Apocalypse, from the creation of man to the Parousia. The Christian liturgy is enraptured with the "admirable exchange" between God and man and the Easter rite celebrates the night "heaven and earth, the divine and the human are joined."

The whole mode of operation of this charity is contained in John's statement: "God is love, and he who abides in love abides in God, and God in him" (1 John 4:16). What this means is that the Father, who is love, makes love descend to men in Christ; Christ in turn jointly sends a new agape, the Holy Spirit; the Father's love, continued in the love of the Father and the Son, takes on an uninterrupted subsistence on earth in the Church, within which men learn to live in love with God and one another. Therefore the Church really constructs herself with love and charity.

When Paul states in his Epistle to the Ephesians that within the Mystical Body there is a diversity of gifts "in order to perfect the saints for a work of ministry, for building up the Body of Christ" (Eph. 4:12), he also later adds: "rather are we to practice the truth in love, and so grow up in all things in him who is the head, Christ. For from him the whole body (being closely joined and knit together through every joint of the system according to the functioning in due measure

184 Cf. mention in A. Beil, *Einheit in der Liebe* (3rd ed. Freiburg im Br., 1955), p. 10.

of each single part) derives its increase to the building up of itself in love" (Eph. 4:15-16). Without charity there is no growth of the Mystical Body; the Church grows only with charity. All ecclesial actions are thus reduced to charity.

Pastoral solicitude is a service of charity. We frequently give an exclusively individual but clerical stamp to apostolic action; we identify pastoral action with priestly action, which is not wholly just.[185] Pastoral action is an ecclesial action, an action of all the members of the Mystical Body of Christ, within which the presbyters have a typically priestly role. This is the New Testament's manner of thought and likewise the way the Church has conceived things from the beginning. Nor have the recent popes forgotten this, although it has not always been present in the thinking of all theologians. The introduction of law into ecclesiology has without a doubt done a great deal of damage not only to pastoral work but to the law itself.

This third ecclesial action, pastoral solicitude, has lived through some bitter moments in the history of the Church. What has happened, in fact, is that this pastoral solicitude has come to be thought of as having just the opposite of its real meaning. As can be seen throughout the history of pastoral work, the Christian paradox about the fact that to rule in the Church is to serve and that to serve is to reign reaches the crisis point as soon as there is not a high level of faith. The Gospel tells us repeatedly that the first should make himself last, and the same message is brought out in all the Epistles.

The defense and guarding of the first two ecclesial

185 Cf. G. M. Brassó, *Liturgia . . .*, *op. cit.*, p. 327: "Indeed, pastoral action — that is, the priestly action upon the faithful. . . ."

actions is easier than the genuine observance of the third. After all, even though the word of God be badly preached, it is substantially contained in the Scriptures, which are clearly and emphatically defined by the Church. Worship, saturated through and through with the Bible, was long ago safeguarded against dangerous improvisations. In fact, according to Jungmann's monumental work, we celebrate the Mass today in a way basically similar to that of the early Christians.

In preaching, the *missio canonica* has often prevailed over really bearing witness and has been reduced to a clerical task at all levels. With regard to worship, the activity of the ministers has frequently forgotten the active participation of the faithful, neglecting at the same time inner devotion, perhaps because of forgetting that the worship of the New Alliance is to "worship the Father in spirit and in truth" (John 4:23). Pastoral solicitude, besides being considered an exclusively priestly job, has often turned into a mere *beneficium* at times, if not a downright *dominium*. Nothing could be more opposed to the *diakonía* of the New Testament.

The word *diakonein*, unknown in the Septuagint, meant in classic Greek to prepare the table, especially for a wedding. In the New Testament the word is used for what amounts to waiting on table (Luke 17:8; John 12:2; Mark 1:31; Matt. 4:11). "The table," according to A. Hamman, "figures as a privileged place where social relations are manifested in the best possible way, as well as for the distance separating the servant from him who is served."[186] Later on this term came to mean different forms of charity, from which one can deduce that pastoral solicitude or charity is an authentic service.

The roots of pastoral solicitude, as an ecclesial action,

186 A. Hamman, "Liturgie et action sociale," *La Maison-Dieu*, XXXIV (1953), 152.

extended back as far as the Incarnation. "Have this mind in you," says Paul, "which was also in Christ Jesus, who though he was by nature God, did not consider being equal to God a thing to be clung to, but emptied himself, taking the nature of a slave and being made like unto men. And appearing in the form of man, he humbled himself, becoming obedient to death, even to death on a cross" (Phil. 2:5-8). This, then, is the one great service, given to us by Christ. After the Last Supper, when His disciples were disputing among themselves as to "which of them was reputed to be the greatest," Jesus Himself said: "I am in your midst as he who serves" (Luke 22:27). It was then that Christ employed the image of the table to impress on them this profound thought which, sad to say, has so often been forgotten since: "let him who is greatest among you become as the youngest, and him who is the chief as the servant" (Luke 22:26). Matthew and Mark tell a similar story before Christ's triumphal entry into Jerusalem, when the sons of Zebedee, urged on by their mother, sought to receive the first places. Jesus answered them by saying: "The Son of Man has not come to be served but to serve, and to give his life as a ransom for many" (Matt. 20:28; Mark 10:45).

Christ's service reaches its fullness on the cross. The sacrifice of Calvary, ritualized in the Eucharistic Supper, is the *diakonía,* Christianity's supreme service of love; rather than the handing over of something, it is the gift of oneself that is expressed in the sacrifice.[187]

To serve as a Christian is in the first place to make Christ's great deaconship reach all men, along with His sacraments. For this reason preaching is the *service of the Word* and the celebration of the mysteries the

187 *Ibid.*, 154.

service of the Table. Both are really a service of Christ, a service of Agape.

It is only natural that charitable service, whose expression lies in solicitude for the poor, should be united to the banquet of the Word and the Sacrament, which is the Mass. The Mass in turn announces and carries out the heavenly banquet of the marriage of the Lamb. In the Mass, which is the greatest of banquets since it gives us Christ, there should be three services present. It is not enough that there be a eucharistic-sacramental service; it is also necessary that there be a complete service of the Word (intelligible proclamation and preaching) and a service of charity (material offering and an embrace or greeting of peace among all participants). The Mass, because it is in the center of pastoral action, divides apostolic work into two main channels. First comes evangelization, which basically consists in proclaiming the message of salvation so that the people may become converted and, once converted, baptized. After the Mass comes all of life, which is an exercise in charity. Between evangelization and charity, in a privileged moment which is the great pastoral *Kairós,* the Christian community celebrates the Eucharist.[188]

The parish is the local eucharistic community that gathers baptized converts to its heart, overflowing with charity. Celebrating the Holy Eucharist with baptized persons who are scarcely converted is as far from the pastoral ideal as celebrating it without charity would be. Just as faith precedes the sacrament, so also the exercise of charity is a consequence. The parish is a local eucharistic community which, with its "Ite missa est" sends forth all its members to live charity intensely. If its members are strangers in a world that does not

188 "Evangélisation et Liturgie," *La Maison-Dieu,* XL (1954), 165-168.

really belong to them, no member of that world, on the other hand, ought to feel like a stranger in the parish, since it is truly a dynamic local community of love.

"Tend the flock of God" (1 Pet. 5:2)

The Church appeared with the sending of the Holy Spirit; with the event of Pentecost the Church began to be an historical reality. The Israelite people, fifty days after celebrating their first Passover, experienced their first Pentecost, sealing at Mount Sinai the great pact of the Covenant. The first Christian group likewise celebrated its first Pentecost with the coming of the Holy Spirit, fifty days after the Savior's resurrection. Moses received the ancient law written on stones; the Apostles, with Mary at their head, wrote the new law on their hearts. Formerly the norm was the law and the prophets; now it was to be the spirit of the Gospel. Everything ended there and everything began with the first coming of the Messiah; everything here will end and everything will begin with the Savior's second coming. On the day of their Passover the Hebrews passed through the waters of the Red Sea, whereas we have been reborn through the waters of Baptism.

In the first Pentecost the Holy Spirit descended, and all those who received Him, since they already formed a Church, were sent forth. But the Church is not a community of indifferent members nor was it so at the start.

"There are varieties of gifts, but the same Spirit," says Paul, "and there are varieties of ministries, but the same Lord; and there are varieties of workings but the same God, who works all things in all. Now the manifestation of the Spirit is given to everyone for profit" (1 Cor. 12:4-6). The two sacramental signs that divide the members of the Christian community are those of Confirmation and the priesthood. Confirmed persons and presbyters form the people of God. In both groups there is the same divine life because the Spirit is one and so is Christ, but their functions are different. There is thus an inequality of functions in the Church but an equality of life. "The *inequality* which produces in some the duty to govern and in others that of obeying," says Mersch, "does not affect however the *equality* which balances them all out in the eyes of the one great Pastor, whose sheep they all are. Ecclesiastical superiors, in fact, are not superior except as public figures; their superiority concerns their function and has nothing to do with their individual lives. They interpret the law of Christ and, it is true, only they have the power to do it, but that law which they alone have interpreted they must also observe along with everyone else. They indeed have at their disposal the means of salvation but just like everyone else they have need of the penitence they preach, the Eucharist if they want to possess life, and Extreme Unction when they die."[189] Augustine stated: "We are Christians for your sake."[190] And he also said: "I am a Christian with you, a bishop for you."[191]

The life of grace is the same for all the members of the Church. These members differ only in their functions. Not even the charisms are a privilege reserved for priests, since they are not necessarily linked to a priestly function. The least known member of the Mystical Body can become an extraordinary charismatic. This simply means that charism is independent of function, not incompatible with it. The fact that "the gates

189 P. Mersch, *Théologie du Corps Mystique*, II, 218; cf. mention in Y. M.-J. Congar, "Le peuple fidèle et la fonction prophétique," *Irénikon*, XXIV (1951), 299.

190 *Serm. inéd.*, s. 17, c. 8; *PL* 46, 880.

191 *Serm.* 340, No. 1; *PL* 38, 1483. Cited in Y. M.-J. Congar, "Le peuple . . ." *op. cit.*, pp. 289-312; 440-466.

of hell shall not prevail against the Church" (Matt. 16:18) and that Jesus Christ will be with the Apostles and with their successors "all days even unto the consummation of the earth" (Matt. 28:20), indicates that in a certain sense charism is connected with ministry, since a Church that developed its whole ministry bureaucratically would not be a Church.

What interests us here is observing the variety in the ministry. In a strict sense there is only one ministry, the priestly one, just as there is only one sacrament of Orders. In this sense, if pastoral action is the exclusive work of priests, we can say it is completely a priestly action. But what about the activity of the confirmed? There is a certain place in the proclamation of the word, and an active place in worship for them; have they no participation in pastoral solicitude?

"The West," Congar tells us, "has separated things. It has dissociated mysticism from thought, reducing the latter to a rationalism which, confining the Church in the category of authority, has led her to juridicism and from there to secularism."[192] Ecclesiastical authority, such as it appears in many theological writings, is closer to civil law than to the *mysterium Ecclesiae*. It has been said that in the Church some have everything and others have hardly anything. "The society which forms the Church," A. Alonso-Lobo has said, "is made up of a double category or class of members essentially different from one another: sacred persons and the plain faithful; those who preach and those who listen; those who govern and those who are governed; clerics and the laity."[193] We do not agree with this way of thinking.

192 Y. M.-J. Congar, "Le peuple . . ." *op. cit.*, p. 310.

193 A. Alonso-Lobo, *¿Qué es y qué no es la Acción Católica?* (Madrid, 1950), p. 23; cf. ref. and reply to this thinking in Fr. Sauras, "El laicado y el poder cultural del sacerdote. ¿Existe un sacerdocio laical?" *Rev. Esp. Teol.*, XIV (1954), 275-326.

The Acts of the Apostles show us a Church in which "all who believe were together and had all things in common" (Acts 2:44). *Life* was the same but it already suggested a *structure,* according to which there were various ministries. Peter was the first to propose (1:15), to proclaim (2:14), to decide (15:7) because he had the primacy; afterwards came the Eleven (2:14), who soon were joined by Paul (9:19, 28). We have already seen how the bishops, presbyters, and deacons came into being.

Primitive patristic teaching, in close contact with apostolic thought, tells us how salvation comes through the Church in the different ecclesial actions, in which all Christians in some way participate. The proclamation of the word is a common task, although not in the same *degree* for everyone; the worship celebration is for everyone but not in the same way. However, the exercise of charity, which is the fullness of Christianity, is for everyone in the same degree and way.[194]

With the sometimes abusive introduction of law into the cure of souls, the third ecclesial action radically changed appearance. It even became separated from preaching and liturgy and ended up reduced to an *officium sacerdotale.* From Christ's triple power as King, Prophet, and Priest it was deduced that this third ecclesial action, derived from Christ's royalty, was a *regere,* a form of government. Since no one delved deeply into the biblical meaning of this action, what prevailed was the juridical, outward, and nonmystical aspect. Today we have once again discovered that evangelical sense, precisely because of studying and clarifying the theology of the laity. The Church is hierarchical not because it is an *imperium* but because it is a *mysterium caritatis;* there are grades or degrees in the Church because it is

194 K. Delahaye, *Erneuerung . . .,* *op. cit.,* p. 184.

an agape, a banquet of charity in which all participate, with some serving more and others less. It is true that laymen must *obey* the hierarchy but it is no less true that the hierarchy ought to *serve.* It is precisely when the pastor of a parish is the *servant* of all that everyone obeys him more eagerly. *Dominium* is perhaps the priestly sin which for parishioners is hardest to forget.

All the Church's members are active and they are active jointly, although not all on the same level or in the same fashion.[195] The strict mission of preaching the word, celebrating worship, and tending God's flock is a priestly one that reaches its fullness if the laymen bear witness to the word they hear, if they actively take part in the worship which the priest directs, and if they respond with evangelical charity to the charity that the Lord's minister incarnates. Because laymen are confirmed, which makes them active members of the Mystical Body, their job is necessary for the growth of the Church. This is so not because priests are sometimes scarce, but for a strictly theological reason. It is precisely when priests are excessively abundant and begin to invade the layman's area, keeping him from coming of age, that the Church runs the risk of inorganic, diseased growth.

"Both the clergy and the laity are sacred, are select," says Father Sauras; "the layman is sacred and select, with a common consecration and selection. Above this there is another, particular selection and consecration, which is what gives rise to the clergy."[196]

The pastor is a priest. Because the seal of the Spirit has been engraved on him in a special way, as distinct from the common seal that all the faithful have received, he solemnly proclaims the word, celebrates the Eucharist

195 Y. M.-J. Congar, "Le peuple . . .," *op. cit.*, p. 442.
196 Sauras, "El laicado . . .," *op. cit.*, p. 285.

as chief minister, and is in his parish the servant of everyone else, since he has received the *officium paroeciale.* Since in the long run all Church action can be reduced to charity, we can say in summary that the parish is the local Christian community served by a priest.

"You are now the people of God" (1 Pet. 2:10)

Pentecost is a paschal plenitude, an effusion of Spirit, a mission; Confirmation in the same way is a baptismal plenitude, a receiving of the Spirit, a sending forth. Just as it is always Pentecost in the Church, so the Christian's life is always a Confirmation. The Church would betray herself if she tried to live with her back turned to Pentecost; a Christian would betray himself and be a traitor to God's people if he tried to turn his back on his Confirmation. Confirmation is each Christian's Pentecost, just as Pentecost is the Church's Confirmation.

"Be you yourselves as living stones," Peter told the converts from paganism, "built thereon into a spiritual house, a holy priesthood, to offer spiritual sacrifices acceptable to God through Jesus Christ. . . . You are a chosen race, a royal priesthood, a holy nation, a purchased people; that you may proclaim the perfections of him who has called you out of darkness into his marvelous light" (1 Pet. 2:5, 9).

Confirmation is a spiritual Baptism. Everything which begins with Baptism reaches maturity in Confirmation; in the first place, incorporation into the people of God, childlike in Baptism and more developed in Confirmation. Although God is the author of both the natural and supernatural orders, this does not mean that the two spheres are strictly parallel. Spiritual maturity can be much more rapid than psychological maturity. Nevertheless, although the sacrament always has an *ex opere operato* force because it is an action of Christ, its *ex opere operantis* dynamism will still depend on the disposition of the person who receives it and possesses it. If baptismal plenitude is not somehow present (faith and conversion), the objective spiritual maturity of Confirmation will not be subjectively manifested. It is for this reason that we have so many confirmed persons who do not bear witness; in their Pentecost they are not now nor have they ever been adequately disposed. Witness is the main effect of Confirmation, since a citizen of the nation of God must act as such. Besides being a "living stone," which is to say a converted and baptized believer, he must "proclaim the perfections" of Christ; herein lies his prophetic mission, closely linked to his inner spiritual life. If his mission is active and his spiritual life profound, his testimony will be complete.

Secondly, Confirmation is the sacrament of the royal priesthood of the faithful. Through Baptism of water the Christian was already incorporated into this priesthood but through Baptism of Spirit his tasks are made concrete. The confirmed person thus has a prophetic dignity and, in a true sense of the word, a priestly dignity. He can offer *spiritual sacrifices.* The assembly of the confirmed forms a Christian community which, under the direction of the officially constituted ministers of worship, will offer the Father the eucharistic sacrifice of Jesus Christ.

Finally, the confirmed man has a royal dignity which proceeds from the royalty of Christ. The Messiah is the Anointed, the Confirmed One, not anointed with the oil of the Kings of Israel but with the Holy Spirit. We have seen that the Kingdom of God is a kingdom of love and that the first in the kingdom is the servant of the rest. To participate in Christ's royalty is to participate in His service of charity. For this reason the pope, from the time of St. Gregory the Great, is called "the servant of the servants of God" because he is the great anointed one of the Church, the visible representation of the Messiah.

"You who in times past were not a people are now the people of God" (1 Pet. 2:10). The parish is a local community of confirmed people, the people of God. The first anointed one of the parish is the pastor, while the bishop is the only one capable of anointing the rest.

We could say that the parish is a local community of the anointed. Their anointing allows them to actively participate in Christ's royalty, in His *deaconship*. Confirmed persons take part in pastoral solicitude in two ways: by receiving a charitable service from the presbyters and bishop, as a people who take their seats at the Kingdom's banquet, and also by serving all their neighbors, whoever they may be, so that no one fails to come to the love feast of the Lamb.

The parish, then, is a local community of confirmed people served by a priest. The whole parish community's task as a living cell of the diocesan Church is a task of charity. First comes inner charity, so that its basis and keystone are Christ: agape incarnate in the fullness of time. Then follows outgoing charity toward all the "lost sheep" so that ". . . by reason of our good works they may glorify God in the day of visitation" (1 Pet. 2:12).

The parish is a community of "strangers and pilgrims" in this world (1 Pet. 2:11), with "no permanent city" but seeking "for the city that is to come" (Hebr. 13:14) until "what is mortal be swallowed up by life" (2 Cor. 5:4). It does not stop where the limits of the Christian community end, but instead includes two other communities through a profound relationship: the human community, in the midst of which the Christian lives, and the heavenly one, the final destination for the human community. With relation to the human family, the Christian community is a missionary group and with respect to the heavenly community it is a band of pilgrims. If the eschatological sense is essential to a parish, the importance of its missionary aspect is no less so. In fact, the more eschatological a parish is—that is, the more spirit of pilgrimage it has—the more missionary it is. And if its feeling that it is a stranger comes from deep down inside the community, the missionary action should proceed from all the members that constitute it.

The parish thus must be missionary with an eschatological sense, without forgetting for a moment that it is the entire Christian community that operates pastorally in the human community until it succeeds in making all those in the community a genuine *communio sanctorum.*

"To him who is able to accomplish all things in a measure far beyond what we ask or conceive, in keeping with the power that is at work in us—to him be glory in the Church and in Christ Jesus down through all the ages of time without end. Amen" (Eph. 3:20-21).

CONCLUSION

Through the preceding pages we have attempted to apply the modern concept of pastoral theology to the ecclesial reality of the parish.

In the first part we analyzed the term "parish" and reached the conclusion that, according to the New Testament, it means the religious community that journeys through the world toward God without any full right to citizenship in this life. Afterwards, the New Testament showed us the character of the primitive apostolic community and the internal laws of its growth.

The fact that the parish has survived down to our times after more than a millennium and a half of existence makes one think that its origin is due to the inner requirements of the growth in history of the people of God. The history of the parish, as we have seen in the second part, is a summarized and valuable history of the Church.

However, neither biblical data nor history is sufficient for developing a theology of the parish. As we have already said, biblical and historical theology, which is to say positive theology, must be accompanied by systematic theology. And we have used the theology of the Church as a starting point for the third part of our work.

The diocese stands midway between the universal Church and the parish. Since the time of Peter the word *ekklesía* has been used to designate the universal Church as well as the local church or diocese. But the Greek word *paroikía* was also applied to the Church with a sense of a pilgrim community with no right of citizenship. Etymologically speaking, the diocese is a local (parochial) pilgrim church, that is to say the pilgrim Church *hic et nunc.*

The Church is not divided as one divides a nation into provinces but instead she *participates* or *concentrates* herself. The universal Church *concentrates* herself in each of her dioceses, presided over by a full priest (the bishop); the local church *participates* in parishes, which are presided over by second-rank priests (pastors). The diocese exists because the celebration of the Eucharist—which is the essence of the Church—is local; the parish exists because the first and most natural means of eucharistic celebration is to be found amid a community of neighbors. The diocese came into being with the Church and the parish was born after the diocese. The diocese is thus of divine law and the parish of ecclesiastical law. The Church is unthinkable without one or more dioceses, but the diocese could exist without parishes. Nevertheless, although the diocese is *essential* to the Church, the parish (as a local eucharistic community) is not accidental to the diocese. We could say scholastically that it is a *proprium,* something that is neither essential nor accidental but which springs from the essence.

The diocese, therefore, is an ecclesial community served by a full priest. It is built up like the Mystical Body: on the altar. All diocesan pastoral work ought to be a *going to the altar* from the word by way of faith, conversion, and the sacraments, and a *coming from the altar* in an intense exercise of charity. The diocese's most privileged moment (its pastoral *kairós*) takes place when its bishop pontifically celebrates the Holy Eucharist with his *presbyterium* and wherever possible his seminarians; surrounding this *kairós* and in intimate communion (let us recall the *fermentum* of the primitive Church) are the parochial *kairoi,* the moments when pastors celebrate the Eucharist with their parishioners. All the notes of the diocesan keyboard sound on the Lord's Day. Sunday is the weekly observance of the paschal feast. It is a part of time which, in the words of Jungmann, thrusts itself into eternity, just as the altar is a piece of stone which finds its way into heaven. *Sunday at the altar:* this is the beginning and the end of all pastoral action. May the pontifical Mass be somehow echoed in the parishes, and the parish Masses be joined to the pontifical Mass. A pontifical Mass without faithful, like a parish church empty at the hour of the people's Mass, is a pastoral tragedy.

But even Sunday, the week's Easter, is in turn subordinate to the great Sunday of the year: the feast of Easter, the feast of feasts. The bishop and his collaborators must cover an entire eucharistic itinerary from Advent to Pentecost if they wish to model the diocese on the image of the Church's mystical Christ. From *kairós* to *kairós,* from Eucharist to Eucharist, toward the great Easter Vigil they must advance in order to descend from that sublime night to the point of departure. Only in this way will we have a diocese and only in this way, too, will we have parishes.

The parish must live on the level of the diocese; it must follow the bishop, the full priest, the way that the conscientious repetition of the new priests rhythmically follows the words that the bishop pronounces at their ordination. In turn, the diocese must live on the level of the Church and follow the universal pastor, the visible figure of Christ.

Then and only then will the diocese be a concentration of the universal Church, and the parish a participation of the local church.

May the Lord be able to say of each one of our dioceses and parishes what He once said of the house that the wise man built: "It did not fall, because it was founded on rock" (Matt. 7:25).

BIBLIOGRAPHY

The parish forms one of the key chapters of pastoral work. More concretely, it is in the parish that the care of souls ordinarily takes place. It is therefore not surprising that the increase in pastoral writings dealing with the parish should have grown so extraordinarily, especially since 1945.

The criterion followed in the preparation of this bibliography has been to be selective while trying not to overlook any of the more important aspects of the parish. The brief notes or explanations which follow most entries, although admittedly personal and incomplete, are an attempt to clarify the value of those works. In order to give a really balanced and impersonal view of the most important works on the parish it would have been necessary to obtain the collaboration of a whole team of experts, as is the case with any undertaking that exceeds the capabilities of a single person.

It may seem strange that the majority of the titles are German and French. For one thing, France and Germany have stayed at the very forefront of writing and thought on the parish. It is always easier for us to be more familiar with what is published within our own countries, above all if this literature is scanty and composed in part of translations. But there is another reason which the most elementary humility cannot hide.

Ortega y Gassett, with his habitual intellectual astuteness, called the district bounded by London, Berlin, Vienna, and Paris the "quadrilateral of science." Pastoral thought, because it is theology, and theology, because it is science, must take into account what is published within this quadrilateral. We know that the "quadrilateral of science" shifts location and is at the mercy of history, but the fact is that there it remains to this very day, in that melting-pot of ideas which is Central Europe. In pastoral matters and therefore with respect to the parish, this melting-pot expresses itself basically in French and in German.

The works in this bibliography have been divided into two main groups: those fashioned jointly by a team, which generally were published for a congress or in a review, and those which are the work of a single author. Analysis of the first group indicates the path that the evolution of the parish concept is following, since it represents a coming together of distinct if not contradictory ways of thinking.

I wish to give my cordial thanks to Father René André, who prepared the French translation of this book, for his help and suggestions in the preparation of this bibliography.

I. Bibliographic Sources

1. Homeyer, J. "Die Erneuerung des Pfarrgedankes. Eine bibliographische Uebersicht," in *Die Pfarre* (No. 22*), 125-158.

An excellent bibliography on the parish; it follows the works' order of appearance within the main parochial fields. It analyzes the best German parish

* This number indicates the place where the work in question appears in this bibliography. The order of the works within each section is that of the date of their publication.

H

literature and gives a sparse sampling of the best works published outside the German-speaking countries.

2. Floristán, C. "Bibliografía sobre la Parroquia," in *La Parroquia, esa vieja novedad,* Madrid: Euramérica, 1958, pp. 483-518.
   Brought up to date and amplified by this present book.
3. Grasso, D. "Osservazioni sulla teologia della parrocchia," *Gregorianum,* XL (1959), 297-314.
   A summary of the main opinions on the parish formulated in recent discussions. A very clear study of the question.
4. Simonet, C. *Théologie de la paroisse.* Paris: Centre de Documentation de l'Union des Oeuvres, 1961. 22 pp. Mimeographed.
   A selection of books and articles, mainly French, about the parish.
5. Liégé, P.-A. "La Paroisse. Bibliographie" in *Parole et Mission,* XX (1963), 109-112.
   A brief but very selective list of works.

II. Collective Works

A. Minutes of Congresses

6. 1946, Besançon, Natl. Congress of the French Union des Oeuvres catholiques. *Paroisse, chrétienté communautaire et missionnaire.* Paris: Fleurus, 1946. 290 pp.
   An excellent presentation, along with Michonneau's book (No. 30), of the community and missionary aspects of the parish.
7. 1948, Lille, Natl. Congress of the French Union des Oeuvres catholiques. *Structures sociales et Pastorale paroissiale.* Paris: Fleurus, 1948. 331 pp.

A magnificent view of the parish's sociological problem, although some very important sociological-religious works have since been published. Congar's paper, "Mission de la paroisse," pp. 48-68, delivered at this Congress, is basic.

8. 1949, Versailles, Session of the Centre de Pastorale Liturgique (C.P.L.) of Paris. "La célébration du culte paroissiale," *La Maison-Dieu,* XX (1950), 3-188.
A required work for understanding the structure of liturgical or para-liturgical parish worship. It follows in the line of the prewar German movement.

9. 1953, Vienna, Week of the Viennese Seelsorgeinstitut (Austrian Pastoral Institute). *Die Pfarre. Gestalt und Sendung.* Vienna: Herder, 1953. 121 pp.
Historical-salvific and theological-kerygmatic type of contribution, especially in the contributions of Schrott and Arnold. This is the Congress which so far has most profoundly studied the parish.

10. 1953, Edmonton, 30th Social Week of the Institut Sociale Populaire of Montreal, Canada. *La paroisse, cellule sociale.* Montreal, 1953. 204 pp.
The Canadian parish has an extraordinary vitality but the minutes of this Congress, even from a sociological point of view, are not very rewarding. They do, however, afford some perspectives not available in the European Congresses.

11. 1954, Bologna, Fourth Natl. Week of "Didascaleion," Milan. *La parrochia. Aspetti pastorali e missionari.* Milan, 1955. 372 pp.
A balanced exposition which follows the line of experimental thought on the parish which originated in postwar France.

12. 1956, Louvaine, V Conférence Internationale de Sociologie Religieuse. *Paroisses urbaines, paroisses*

rurales. Tournai: Casterman, 1958. 224 pp.

13. 1957, Zaragoza, Diocesan Week of the Centro de Estudios Pastorales. *La Parroquia, esa vieja novedad*. Madrid: Euramérica, 1958. 518 pp.
Although its scientific level is generally low, the overall view of the parish is ambitious. Useful as an introduction.
14. 1958, Zaragoza, First Natl. Spanish Parish Week. *Comunidad cristiana parroquial*. Madrid: Euramérica, 1959. 598 pp.
These minutes have a double advantage over the previous ones: fewer themes and more profoundly developed ones. We consider this work to be of real interest. Some contributions, as for example those of Arnold and Martimort, are excellent. Hombría's is also worthy of mention.
15. 1961, Paris, VI Congrès National de l'Union des Religieuses Educatrices Paroissiales. *Aujourd'hui la paroisse*. Paris: Fleurus, 1963. 246 pp.
A good contribution to literature on the parish, theologically as well as practically.
16. 1961, Lausanne, I Colloque Européen des Paroisses. *Situation de la Paroisse: Essais de diagnostic et de réflexion*. Paris: Association Philippe Néri, 1962. pro ms.
17. 1962, Barcelona, III Semana Nacional de la Parroquia. *La Acción Católica y el apostolado seglar en la Parroquia. Apostolado Sacerdotal,* May-June, 1962, pp. 1-159.
The texts of contributions to this Congress, in general of an uneven quality, are in summary form. The majority are of minor value.
18. 1963, Vienna, II Colloque Européen des Paroisses. "Pastorale des marginaux," *Paroisse et Mission,* XX (1964), 1-116.

B. Works in Collaboration

Pastoral works in collaboration not forming part of a congress are widespread in Germany. Naturally, most of them are special issues of magazines or reviews, a trend which is becoming more and more pronounced. It is true that the quality differs considerably, as is true in congresses also, but the contrasts of different perspectives and dialogues are most enlightening. French works of this sort tend to add an extraordinarily valuable résumé or conclusions. This is a touch generally lacking in other countries, perhaps because they lack the typical French quality of exposition with an eye for synthesis. Analysis is more profound in the German works.

19. *Volksliturgie und Seelsorge. Ein Werkbuch zur Gestaltung des Gottesdienstes in der Pfarrgemeinde,* ed. by K. Borgmann. Kolmar, 1942. 188 pp.
A serious attempt at comparing the theoretical and practical results of the liturgical movement. Articles by Guardini, Jungmann, Gülden, Kahlefeld, etc.

20. *Parochia. Handreichung für die Pfarrseelsorge,* ed. by K. Borgmann. Kolmar: Alsatia, 1943. 408 pp.
This can be considered a continuation of the preceding.

21. *Pfarrgemeinde und Pfarrgottesdienst. Beitrage zu Fragen der ordentlichen Seelsorge,* ed. by A. Kirchgassner. Freiburg im Br., 1949. 124 pp.
A comparison of theories and practices about parish liturgy, centering on Sunday Mass.

22. "La comunitá parrocchiale," *Vita Sociale,* IX (1952), 1-96.

23. "La parrocchia e l'apostolato dei laici," *Quaderni Tabor,* III (1952), 5-284.

24. "La parrocchia. Miscellanea di studi in onore del

Card. A. Schuster," *La Scuola Cattolica,* LXXX (1953), special issue.
Of these three Italian works, the issue of *La Scuola Cattolica* is the best and perhaps the best thing published in Italy on the parish to date. The issue of *Tabor* is in general superficial.

25. "Problemes de la Paroisse," *La Maison-Dieu,* XXXVI (1953), 3-150. Contains the text of the letter sent by then-Cardinal Montini to the Canadian Social Week. This letter is not only the best part of the issue, but the best of the whole Canadian Congress.
26. *Die Pfarre. Von der Theologie zur Praxis,* ed. by H. Rahner. Freiburg im Br.: Lambertus Verlag, 1956. 158 pp.
A collection of lectures given by the Jesuits of Innsbruck. Karl Rahner's is outstanding for its profundity; Kahlefeld's is also outstanding.
27. "Paroisse et Mission," *Parole et Mission,* XX (1963), 23-112.
A critical examination of the missionary aspect of the parish. With bibliography.
28. *La paroisse se cherche.* St. Andrew's Abbey, Bruges: Biblica, 1963. 160 pp.
An original and profound comparison of historical, sociological, and theological facts regarding the parish.

III. Individual Works

A. A General View of the Parish

29. Noppel, C. *Die neue Pfarrei, Eine Grundlegung.* Freiburg im. Br.: Herder, 1939. 232 pp. (Italian tr., *La nuova parrocchia.* Turin: L.I.C.E., 186 pp.)
This book has become a classic like those of Michon-

neau and Ryckmans. It is a well-balanced résumé of the state of affairs in Germany in the year 1939. The struggle between proponents of the parish apostolate and supporters of supra-parochial missions was very acute in Germany. The Nazi prohibition of organizations, coupled with the impossibility of eliminating the parishes, indirectly inclined apostolic orientation toward the parish.

30. Michonneau, G. *Parroquia comunidad misionera.* Buenos Aires: Desclée, 1951. 364 pp.
Because of its translation into various languages, this marvellous theoretical-practical exposition has been of great influence in recent years. Its conception, based on practice, is that of a profound pastoral theology. It is an extraordinary contribution since it originates not in some theologian's logical mind but in the experience of a parish team. This is a book for reading, study, and meditation.

31. Feltin, Maurice Card. "Quelques réflexions sur la paroisse," *La Maison-Dieu,* IX (1947), 104-112.
Cardinal Feltin's well-balanced theological and pastoral judgment on the extremely difficult care of souls in Paris is plain to see in these reflections, the result of much reading and meditation. This work is a summary of the parish problem.

32. Peralta, F. *La estructura moderna de la parroquia en sus lineas fundamentales.* Zaragoza, Seminario Metropolitano, 1949.

33. Ryckmans, A. *La parroquia viviente.* Bilbao: Desclée, 1953. 236 pp.
Another important contribution arising out of experience. A profound understanding of the traditional apostolate.

34. Viviani, G. *La parroquia. Reflexiones sobre prob-*

lemas de actualidad. Citta del Vaticano, 1950. 174 pp.

35. Beguiristain, S. *Por esos pueblos de Dios.* Bilbao: Desclée, 1953.
From the aspect of the care of souls, this book is perhaps the most important Spanish contribution to the parish. Its chapters on pastoral ideas for the parish are optimistically written with no attempt at a critical approach. This is a work aimed at the zealous and idealistic young priest, for whom it can be immensely helpful.
36. Blieweiss, Th. *Seelsorge in der Pfarre. Erkenntnisse und Erfahrungen eines Grosstadtsseelsorgers.* Graz: Styria, 1953. 303 pp.
The experiences of a great Viennese pastor.
37. Maduere, S.P. de la. *Regards sur la paroisse. Un effort de réalisme.* Paris: Fleurus, 1956. 200 pp.
Reflections of a Parisian pastor.
38. Heenan, J. C. *El Párroco y su pueblo.* Barcelona: ELE, 1958. 298 pp.
39. "La paroisse," No. CXXXII of *Fêtes et Saisons* (Feb., 1959).
A magnificent model which can serve as the basis for explaining the concept of the parish to the people. It was prepared by the Centre de Pastorale Liturgique of Paris and illustrated under the direction of Father Fleuret.
40. Wimmer, O. *Handbuch der Pfarrseelsorge und Pfarrverwaltung.* Innsbruck: Tyrolia, 1959. 248 pp.
This exhaustive work comprises all of parochial pastoral work, divided into three sections: preaching of the word, celebration of worship, and care of the parish.
41. Rusch, P. *Kirche im Gebirge und Anderswo.* Innsbruck: Tyrolia, 1959. 259 pp.

Wise and profound hints for general pastoral action and parish work, written by the Bishop of Innsbruck.

42. Floristán, C. "La Parroquia en el pensamiento de la moderna pastoral," *Orbis Catholicus,* III (1960), 110-124.
This article corresponds to that part of the present book that analyzes theological opinions on the parish in recent debates.

43. Concha, V. G. de la. *La realidad teológica de la Parroquia.* Oviedo: Metropolitan Seminary, 1960. 87 pp.
Another work examining opinions most in vogue today. Its conclusions coincide with those which we hold, based on the thinking of Congar, Rahner, and Arnold.

44. Morcillo, C. *La Iglesia diocesana y sus parroquias.* Barcelona: Flors, 1960. 210 pp.

45. Tarancon, V. E. *La Parroquia, hoy.* Salamanca: Sígueme, 1961. 309 pp.
Clear and precise pastoral orientations applied to the parish.

46. Rovira, J. *Por una renovación de la Parroquia.* Barcelona: Estela, 1961.
An original and profound view of the parish apostolate, from a practical angle.

47. Blöchlinger, A. *Die Heutige Pfarrei als Gemeinschaft.* Einsiedeln: Benziger Verlag, 1962. 337 pp.
This is the most important and most complete German contribution about the parish. The first part is a historical study, the second part is a profound examination of the parochial community—from the viewpoints of law, theology, liturgy, and sociology—and the third part contains some conclusions.

48. Bailby, P. *El párroco y su parroquia.* Andorra: Casal y Vall, 1962. 134 pp.
A practical essay with little theological cohesion.

B. Specialized Aspects

The Austrian historian Schrott maintains that history is the mother and teacher of pastoral action. The salvation message is deeply immersed in human history. In fact, the Bible is salvation-history and the liturgy is a repetition of that history. Moreover, Christianity is history because it is drama before being doctrine. However, it is not history made by man alone but rather by the special plan of God. The doctrine of the Church cannot be understood without understanding its history. Let us first look at some works dealing with the word "parish."

1. Meaning of the word.

49. Stolz, E. "*παροικία,* parochia und parochus," *Tübinger Theologische Quartalschrift,* LXXXIX (1907), 424-448.
Ibid. "Zur Geschichte des Terminus Parochus," *ibid.,* XCV (1913), 193-203.
Ibid. "Parochus," *ibid.,* CVII (1926), 1-8.
These three works, although relatively old, have become classics in their field. They scientifically clarify for us the origin of the terms "parish" and "pastor."

52. Schmitt, K. L., "*πάροικος, παροικία, πάροικέω,*" etc. (Ger.) *Theologisches Wörterbuch zum Neuen Testament,* ed. by Kittel (1954), 840-852.
Following the same method that Kittel introduced so revolutionarily in his famous dictionary, Schmitt studies the three concepts from pagan antiquity to

apostolic times. Blöchlinger's work (No. 47) contains valuable indications of the origin of these concepts.

2. History of the Parish

53. Imbart de la Tour, P. *Les paroisses rurales dans l'ancienne France du IV au VI siécle.* Paris: Picard, 1900.
Despite the date of its publication, this is still a standard reference work.
54. Zorell, St. "Die Entwicklung des Parochialsystems bis zum Ende der Karolingerzeit," *Archiv für Kirchenrecht,* LXXXII (1902), 74-98, 258-289.
55. Berliere, U. "L'exercice du ministère paroissial par les moines dans le haut moyen âge," *Rév. bénéd.,* XXXIX (1927), 227-250.
56. Bidagor, R. *La "Iglesia propia" en España.* A historical canonical study. Rome: Univ. Greg., 1933. 176 pp.
57. Seaton, W. "Note sur les origines religieuses des paroisses rurales," *Rev. Hist. Ph. Relig.,* XV (1935), 243-354.
58. Leclercq, H. "Paroisses rurales," in *Dict. d'arch. chrét. et de liturgie,* XIII (1938), col. 2198-2235.
59. Bardy, G. "Sur l'origine des paroisses," *Masses Oeuvrieres,* XXI (1947), 42-59; XXII (1947), 42-66.
60. Adam, P. "La vie paroissiale en France au XIV siècle (1331-1414)." A thesis presented at the University of Strasbourg.
61. Schrott, A. *Seelsorge im Wandel der Zeiten.* Graz: Styria, 1949. 225 pp.
62. *Ibid.* "Pfarre und Pfarrseelsorge im Wandel der Zeiten," in *Die Pfarre* (No. 9), 9-17.
The above two works give an excellent synthesis

of the history of the parish. The preceding ones, which analyze historical parish aspects, contribute to an overall view, although some concentrate on canonical evolution.

63. Monachino, V. *La cura pastorale a Milano, Cartagine e Roma nel sec. IV*. Rome: Univ. Greg., 1947. 442 pp.

64. Nanni, L. *La parrocchia studiata nei documenti lucchesi dei secoli VIII-XIII*. Rome: Univ. Greg., 1948. 231 pp.

65. Beck, G. J. H. *The Pastoral Care of Souls in South-East France during the Sixth Century*. Rome: Univ. Greg., 1950. 415 pp.

66. Fernández Alonso, J. *La cura pastoral en la España romanovisigótica*. Rome: I.E.E.E., 1955. 628 pp.

These last four works, published at the Gregorian University, mark a trend in Church history toward the study of her inner life. Fernández Alonso's thesis will be a required reference work for quite some time to come in order to understand this important stage of the Spanish Church.

67. Nanni, L. "L'evoluzione storica della Parrocchia," *La Scuola cattolica*, LXXXI (1953), 475-544.

68. Nanni, L. "Lo sviluppo storico della parrocchia e i suoi insegnamenti," in *La Parrocchia. Aspetti pastorali e missionari*, XI, 62-75.

These two works of Nanni's, along with that of Schrott (No. 62) are magnificent résumés of parish history.

69. Griffe, E. "Les paroisses rurales de la Gaule," in *La Maison-Dieu*, XXXVI (1953), 33-62.

A historical study covering the period from the foundation of the parish, in the fourth century, to the Carolingian era.

70. Beauduin, L. "L'esprit paroissial dans la Tradition,"

in *Mélanges liturgiques*. Louvain: Mont-César, 1954. pp. 229-256.

71. Broutin, P. "Histoire et tradition pastorales," in *Nouv. Rev. Théol.*, LXXVII (1955), 725-736.
72. Le Bras, G. *Introduction à l'histoire de la pratique religieuse en France*. Paris: P.U.F., 2 vol., 1942 and 1945. 128 and 152 pp.
73. *Ibid. Etudes de Sociologie religieuse*. Paris: P.U.F., 2 vol., 1955-56. 815 pp.
These four volumes by Le Bras are not only the best works written to date on religious sociology, they constitute a source of profound meditation for Church historians and canonists. He proposes to historians that they undertake research on little-known religious practices, and he makes canonists see that the Code of Canon Law is not all-important. Le Bras' books are works which join a concrete and precise view of a problem to the universal vision of a deeply scientific and Catholic teacher.
74. Broutin, P. *La Réforme Pastorale en France au XVII siècle*. Tournai: Desclée et Cie, 1956. 2 vols., 372 and 567 pp.
A well-documented historical work.
75. Arnold, F.-X. *Al servicio de la fe. Ensayo de pastoral catequética*. Span. transl. Buenos Aires: Herder, 1960. 82 pp.
76. *Ibid. Grundsätzliches and Geschichtliches zur Theologie der Seelsorge*. Freiburg im Br.: Herder, 1949. 171 pp.
77. *Ibid. Mensaje de fe y comunidad cristiana. Contribución a una teología del Mensaje, de la Parroquia y del Laicado*. Estella: Verbo Divino, 1961. (Translation of section of No. 9 above.)
78. *Ibid. Seelsorge aus der Mitte der Heilsgeschichte*. Freiburg im Br.: Herder, 1956.

These four works mark a new stage in modern European pastoral action. The first one was decisive in the publication of the new German catechism. Arnold's most notable characteristic is his sense of salvation history, so characteristic of the famous Tübingen school. He always attacks pastoral technology and looks for the principles of biblical theology developed by tradition—above all by patristics—and expressed by the great era of scholasticism. He is a profound student of the Protestant schism and extremely cautious in judging the Church's pastoral tradition from the fourteenth century to our day. The third item (No. 77) includes Arnold's magnificent work on the parish.

79. Schmitt, Th.-J. *L'organisation ecclésiastique et la pratique religieuse dans l'archidiaconé d'Autun de 1650 à 1750.* Autun: Marcelin, 1957. 374 pp.
80. Voosen, E. "Origine des paroisses: causes et occasions," *Revue diocésaine de Namur,* XIII (1959), 51-60.
81. Böhm, F. *Parochie und Gemeinde im 19. und 20. Jahrhundert.* Marburg/Lahn, 1958.
82. Pinckers, Gh. "Eglise locale et évangélisation," in *La paroisse se cherche* (No. 28), 71-107.

3. The Parish, Mystical Reality

In recent years the liturgists have developed the parish's mystical aspect, and the religious sociologists have examined the parish's social body. Out of the meeting between these two perspectives there has grown up an authentic conception of the parish.

a) Theological aspect

83. Lesêtre, H. *La paroisse.* Paris: Lecoffre, 1906. 263 pp.

84. Congar, Y. "Mission de la paroisse," in *Structures* (No. 7), 48-65. Congar's is a sensible and well-balanced evaluation of the prewar German pastoral movement. From a theological viewpoint it is an essential contribution.
85. Spiazi, R. "Spunti per una Teologia della parrocchia," *La Scuola cattolica,* LXXX (1952), 26-42.
86. Ceriani, G. "La Parrocchia: rilievi dogmatici e giuridici," in *La Parrocchia* (No. 11), 76-107.
Italian thought on the parish is neither so theologically sound as the German nor so sociologically energetic as the French. The influence of canon law, so characteristic of the Italians, makes it difficult for them to see the parish reality either with a great mystical purity or as a simple social body, omitting the juridical consideration.
87. Arnold, F.-X. "Zur Theologie der Pfarrei," in *Die Pfarre,* (No. 9), 18-36.
88. Rahner, K. "Zur Theologie der Pfarrei," in *Die Pfarre,* (No. 26), 27-40.
From the theological point of view, these two lectures, along with Congar's, are the best works on the parish published in recent years. Arnold's is the most complete, Rahner's is very profound, and Congar's is full of suggestions. All three are indispensable.
89. Chappoulie, Msgr. *La paroisse dans l'Eglise.* Paris: F.N.A.C., 1953.
90. Montini, G.-B. "La paroisse dans l'Eglise. Lettre du août 1953 à la semaine sociale du Canada." *La Maison-Dieu,* XXXVI (1953), 9-13.
91. "La paroisse, Fiche de Travail," in *Masses Oeuvrières,* LXXXIII (1953), 4 pp.
92. Michonneau, G. *Le curé.* Paris: Fayard, 1954. 192 pp.

93. Jenny, H. "Qu'est-ce qu'une paroisse?" in *Equipes Enseignantes,* 3rd quarter, 1954-1955.
94. Guzzetti, G. B. "La Parrocchia," in *La Scuola Cattolica,* LXXXII (1954), 292-303.
95. Ryckmans, A. "Notes de théologie pastorale. Pour une théologe de la paroisse," *Nouv. Rev. Théol.,* LXXVI (1954), 524-527.
96. Floristán, C. "Hacia una nueva concepción de la parroquia," in *La parroquia, esa vieja novedad,* (No. 13) 57-80, and in *Lumen* VII (1958), 97-120 under the title: "Concepto que hoy tenemos de la parroquia."
This report at the Zaragoza Diocesan Week sums up the problematic discussion on the parish up to 1957.
97. Denis, H. "La paroisse," fiche théologique No. 18 in the *Semaine religieuse de Lyon,* March 28, 1958.
98. Decourtray, A. "Théologie de la paroisse et pastorale paroissiale," in *L'Union,* 744 (1959), pp. 9-18; 745 (1959), 17-24.
99. Charue, A.-M. "Paroisse et théologie," *Revue diocésaine de Namur,* I (1961), 1-17.
100. Schruers, P. "Théologie de la paroisse," *Revue Ecclésiastique de Liége,* XLIX (1963), 168-178.
101. Frisque, J. "La paroisse, centre d'evangélisation," in *La paroisse se cherche* (No. XXVIII), 141-158.

b) Liturgical aspect

102. Wintersig, A. "Pfarrei und Mysterium," *Jahrbuch für Liturg.,* V (1925), 136-143. (French trans., "Le réalisme mystique de la paroisse," *La Maison-Dieu,* VIII [1946], 15-26.)
103. Pinsk, J. "Die religiöse Wirklichkeit von Kirche, Diözese und Pfarrei," in *Der kathol. Gedanke,* VI

(1933), 337-344. (French transl., in *Les Quest. Lit. et Par.*, XVIII, 192-205.)

104. Parsch, P. "Die Pfarre als Mysterium," in *Die lebendige Pfarrgemeinde,* the Vienna Congress of 1933, Seelsorger-Sonderheft (1934), 13-33.
105. Schurr, M. "Die Uebernatürliche Wirklichkeit der Pfarrei," in *Benediktinische Monatsschrift,* XIX (1937), 81-106.
These four articles mark the high-water point of liturgical advance in the prewar German parish, to the degree that they almost ignore the social aspect.
106. Valpertz, L. "Liturgische Arbeit in der Pfarrgemeinde," in *Theologie und Glaube,* XXIX (1937), 548-556.
Follows the same line as the foregoing.
107. Morin, G. *Pour un renouveau liturgique paroissial.* Paris: Cerf, 1944. 76 pp.
108. Flacelière, R. *Renouveau paroissial et vie liturgique.* Paris: Seuil, 1945.
109. Tonolo, Fr. *Parrocchia liturgica.* Rome: 1949.
110. Conclusions of the Session at Versailles "La célébration du culte paroissial," *La Maison-Dieu,* XX (1950), 187-188.
This whole Congress is highly important and its conclusions are extraordinarily valuable.
111. Feltin, M. Card. *La messe de la paroisse.* Lyon: Ed. de l'Abeille, 1952. 68 pp.
112. Himmer, Ch. M., Bishop of Tournai. "La messe et de paroisse," (Lent, 1956), *Quest. Lit. et Par.,* XXXVI (1955), 315-324.
These two works are pastoral letters of a high value.
113. Mayer, J. E. *Das liturgische Leben der Pfarre,* in *Die Pfarre* (No. 9), 62-70.

114. Jungmann, J. A. "Die Liturgie im Leben der Pfarre," in *Die Pfarre* (No. 26), 67-74.
These last two works are representative of parish liturgical thought in the German Federal Republic and Austria. Jungmann also made a noteworthy contribution in 1938 with his essay, "Die liturgische Feier" (The Laws of Liturgical Celebration). This last lecture of his is good but not extraordinary. Its value lies in the fact that it was delivered by a great teacher.

115. Sauras, E. "La Eucharistía y el misterio de la comunidad litúrgica," *Teologia Espiritual,* II (1958), 359-394.

116. Miranda, F., "La liturgia parroquial," in *Comunidad cristiana parroquial* (No. 14), 89-122.

117. Chéry, H. Ch. *Comunidad parroquial y Liturgia.* Span. transl. Bilbao: Desclée, 1959. 187 pp.
One of the first great French experiences of the parish liturgical apostolate.

118. Crichton, J. D. "The Parish," *Liturgy,* XXIX (1960), 1-4; 28-32; 53-60.
A study of the parish viewing it from the angle of assembly of the people of God, assembly of worship and witness.

c) Community aspect

The idea of parish community, discovered and developed in Germany, has been vigorously presented in France at the Congress of Besançon and in the writings of Michonneau. Today it is practiced more in France than in Germany, although the Germans are the leaders in team research.

119. Blieweiss, Th. *Zum aufbau unserer Pfarrgemeinde.* Vienna: Herder, 1940. 72 pp.

120. Metzger, K. *Der Hirt im Aufbau der Gemeinde.* Vienna: Herder, 1948. 15 pp.
Two treatments of the community problem by a pair of well-known Austrian pastors. Their value comes from the priests' parish experience.

121. Schurr, V. "Die Pfarrei als Liebesbund," *Anima,* VIII (1953), 173-177.
Schurr never neglects in his works the concrete situation. He occupies an outstanding place in the German pastoral field today.

122. Michonneau, G. *Pas de vie chrétienne san communauté.* Paris: Cerf, 1960. 156 pp.
This magnificent book reflects Michonneau's fifteen years of experience in three different parishes. Through theological and practical references it brings out the irreplaceable value of community in Christian life.

123. Pin, E. "Can the Urban Parish be a Community?" in *Gregorianum,* XLI (1960), 393-423.
This work demonstrates that the majority of urban parishes are not true spiritual communities. It is an important sociological analysis.

124. Martimort, A.-G. "L'Assemblée liturgique," *La Maison-Dieu,* XX (1950), 153-175.

125. *Ibid.,* "L'Assemblée liturgique, mystère du Christ," *La Maison-Dieu,* XL (1954), 5-29.

126. *Ibid.,* "Aspects théologiques: Dimanche, assemblée, paroisse," *La Maison-Dieu,* LVII (1959), 55-84.

127. *Ibid.,* "Précisions sur l'assemblée," LX (1959), 7-34.

128. *Ibid.,* "L'Assemblée," in *L'Eglise en prière. Introduction a la Liturgie.* Paris: Desclée, 1961. 82-111.
In these five works Martimort has demonstrated a great theological penetration with regard to the theme of the assembly.

129. Misser, S. "Por una pastoral de comunidad. Hacia la parroquia comunitaria," in *Orbis Catholicus,* V. (1962), 502-542.
An excellent presentation of the problem.

d) Missionary aspect

130. *Orientations des missions paroissiales.* Lyón: Chalet, 1947. 138 pp.
131. Lechner, K. *Pfarre und Laie.* Vienna: Herder, 1949, 84 pp.
132. Fischer, E. "Die missionarische Pfarre," in *Die Pfarre* (No. 9), 83-103.
An explanation of the French missionary problem in Vienna, a problem of great interest in German-speaking regions in recent years.
133. Coninck, L. de. "La Paroisse vivante," in *Nouv. Rev. Théol,* LCCIV (1952), 64-66.
134. Hoyois, G. "Les laics dans la paroisse," *La Revue Nouvelle,* XVI (1952), 505-518.
135. Ceriani, G. "Sacerdoti e Laici nella parrocchia," *Tabor,* VI (1952), 51-67.
136. Motte, J. F. "Les missions paroissiales et l'oeuvre de rechristianisation," in *La Maison-Dieu,* XL (1954), 118-135.
137. Michalon, P. "Les communautés primitives d'après les livres du Nouveau Testament," *Masses Oeuvrières,* XCV (1954), 33-51.
138. Houtart, F. "Faut-il abandonner la paroisse dans la ville moderne?" *Nouv. Rev. Théol.,* LXXVII (1955), 602-613.
Missionary methods are necessary in order to respond to the new apostolic problems of the big city.
139. Chapoulie, H. "La paroisse, communauté missionnaire," in *Luttes de l'Eglise,* I. Paris: Fleurus, 1957.

140. Daniel, Y. "Notre paroisse, mystère de salut," *Masses Oeuvrières,* CLVI (1959), 48-62.
141. Hamer, J. "Vocation catholique de la paroisse, sa mission dans l'Eglise," *Evangeliser,* XIV (1960), 21-22.
142. Frisque, J. "Pour une théologie des rapports entre la mission et la paroisse," *La Revue Nouvelle,* XXXV (1962), 579-592.
The dynamism of the eucharistic celebration requires that the parish be truly missionary.
143. Lacorre, G. "Pour des communautés paroissiales en état de mission," *Parole et Mission,* XIX (1962), 605-624.
An important survey analysis.
144. Jubany, N. "La parroquia y la obra de evangelización," *Orbis Catholicus,* V (1962), 97-121.
An excellent synthesis.
145. Liégé, P.-A. "La paroisse era-t-elle missionnaire?" *Parole et Mission,* XX (1963), 39-54.
A study of the parish as a missionary community, in the light of ecclesiology.

e) Biblical aspect

Through Protestant influence, German Catholic theologians have gone deeply into biblical studies. The parish is not of divine origin but the first Christian community was. This accounts for the importance of Bible study in learning about the nature of the first Christian communities.

146. Kirchgässner, A. "Das Bild der Germeinde im Johannesevangelium," in *Pfarrgemeinde und Pfarrgottesdienst* (No. 21), 53-60.
This work initiated the subject and established certain fundamentals, taken from John's Gospel.

147. Josefcyk, A. *A Modern Parish as Modelled on the Life of the Cenacle.* Fribourg (Switz.): Impr. St. Paul, 1951.
A doctoral thesis that studies the basic lines of the parish from the viewpoint of the essential characteristics of the Cenacle. It contributes no fundamental elements but is a very helpful work nonetheless.

148. Wurbel, W. *Bibelarbeit in der Pfarre.* 1955. 110 pp.
Properly speaking this is a study of the parish biblical apostolate.

149. Stöger, A. *Dienst am Glauben. Die Gemeinde und ihr Seelsorger nach dem Philipperbrief.* Munich: 1956.

150. Kahlefeld, H. "Das Leben der Gemeinde nach dem Neuen Testament," in *Die Pfarre,* (No. 26), 41-66.
A splendid résumé of the community problem in the New Testament.

151. Gantoy, R. "La asamblea en la economía de la salvacion" in *Asambleas del Señor,* I. Madrid: Marova, 1964, pp. 56-82.

152. Maertens, Th. *L'assemblée.* Bruges: St. Andrew's Abbey, 1964. 102 pages. Multicopied.
These last two works are notable biblical contributions of great importance to the theme of the assembly; the second of the two is especially original and substantial.

4. The Parish, Social Reality

The advent of religious sociology in the parish has been producing abundant fruits over the past few years. Le Bras was the father of the new science, while Boulard, Lebret and others have been its popularizers. Since 1945—though the origins of this approach go back as far as 1931—a field full of possibilities has been opened up. (Cf. C. Floristán, *La vertiente pastoral de la sociología religiosa.* Vitoria: Eset, 1960. 294 pp.)

a) Sociological View

We first of all list those works of pure methodology, and afterwards those that can serve as models of concrete research. In both cases, the French-speaking countries lead the list by a good margin.

General Methodology

"Structure Sociales . . ." (No. 7), especially the contribution of Le Bras, Lebret, Folliet and Dagallier, can serve as an introduction to the subject.

153. Légaré, H. "Introduction à la sociologie paroissiale," mimeographed thesis. Lille: 1950, 415 pp.
The first major attempt at a parish methodology.
154. Clarke, Th. *Parish Sociology.* Washington: 1945.
155. Nuesse, C. J. & Harte, Th. J. *The Sociology of the Parish. A Survey of the Parish in its Constants and Variables.* Milwaukee: The Bruce Publishing Co., 1951. 354 pp.
American religious sociology forms a school all by itself, distinct from the French school. As yet it does not appear to have reached the level of American sociology generally. The Americans do insist, however, upon being scientific sociologists and not theologians. There are three stages distinguishable: gathering of statistics, analysis of social groups, and preparation of extensive generalizations. European religious sociology seems to dwell on the first stage and has not yet reached the final one.
156. Borlée, L. "Structures sociales et ministère paroissial," *Rev. Dioc. de Tournai,* VI (1951), pp. 427-446.

157. Falardeau, J. Ch. *Sociologie de la paroisse.* Montreal: 1953. Canadian religious sociology studies are more tuned to the French-Belgian school than to the American school.

158. Rimoldi, A. "L'indagine sociologica di una parrocchia," in *La Scuola cattolica,* LXXXI (1953), 439-454.

159. Azzali, I. *L'indagine sociologica di una parrocchia.* Cremona: Pizzorni, 1954. 117 pp.
Both of these studies provide helpful orientations; the former contains an extensive bibliography.

160. Chombart de Lauwe, P. H. *La pratique religieuse dominicale. Etude methodologique.* Centr. de Docum. Univers., Paris, 1954. 32 pp.

161. Fichter, J. H. *Social Relations in the Urban Parish.* Chicago: University of Chicago Press, 1954. 264 pp.

162. *Ibid. Southern Parish,* vol. 1: *The Dynamics of a City Church.* Univ. of Chicago Press, 1951. 284 pp. Fichter is without a doubt the most outstanding American researcher in the field of religious sociology. He is head of the Sociology Department at Loyola University in New Orleans and follows the line of U.S. sociology but is in his own right a profound and original thinker; his works are required reading as complements to European writings. According to his own admission, Protestant religious sociology is farther advanced in the U.S. than its Catholic counterpart, a situation which is just the contrary of that in Europe.

163. Jammes, J. M. *Enquête pastorale: Questionnaire pour l'étude d'une paroisse en pays rural.* Monde, 1955. 32 pp.

164. Greinacher, N. *Soziologie der Pfarrei.* Freiburg: Alsatia, 1955, 309 pp.

An exhaustive study of parochial methodology following the French school.

165. Boulard, F. *L'étude d'une paroisse rurale.* Voiron: S.A.G.M.A., 1956.
A highly valuable sociological instrument from the hand of a master.

166. Pin, E. *Introduction a l'étude sociologique de paroisses catholiques.* Paris: Action Popul., 1956. 168 pp.
The Jesuit Father Pin has in just a short time advanced to the first ranks of religious sociology through his deep capacity for reflection. This book on parish methodology and typology is excellent.

167. Goldschmidt, D., Greiner, F. & Schelsky, H. *Soziologie der Kirchengemeinde,* Stuttgart: 1960.
A joint work of broad scope.

168. Carrier, H. *Psycho-sociologie de l'appartenance religieuse.* Rome: Gregorian Univ., 1960. 314 pp.
An original and profound study.

169. De Smedt, E. *Le Christ dans le quartier. Pour un renouveau de la paroisse urbaine.* Paris-Bruges: Desclée de Br., 1960. 144 pp.

170. Daniel, Y. "Découverte sociologique d'une paroisse et ses incidences pastorales," *Paroisse et Mission,* XI (1960), 26-56.

171. Pin, E. "La sociologie de la paroisse," in *Situation de la paroisse* (No. 16).

172. Houtart, F. "Pastorale missionnaire et paroissiale dans les grandes villes," *Parole et Mission,* XX (1963), 55-78.

173. Houtart, F. "Sociologie de la paroisse comme assemblée eucharistique," in *La paroisse se cherche* (No. 28), 109-126.

Concrete Examples

In almost all these examples, the parish is the basic experimental cell. We also list here research on whole zones and regions.

174. Clemens, J. "Eine Grosstadtpfarrei nach dem Kriege," *Stimmen der Zeit,* CXLIII (1949), 366-376 pp.
One of the first German studies of a city parish. It lacks the modern French precision. On the whole the German Church possesses religious statistics as does no other country, but because of the German suspicion of statistics in religious matters, they have scarcely been used in pastoral work there.

175 Petit, J. "Structure sociale et pratique religieuse dans la paroisse Saint-Laurent," Paris: 1950. 102 pp. (unpublished). A summary of this important work is to be found in *Archives des Religions* I (1956), 71-127.

176. Censi, M. A. "Una indagine campione in una parroccchia urbana," *Orientamenti Sociali,* IX (1953), 11-24 pp.
An outstanding contribution by an Italian religious.

177. Chelini, J. *Genèse et évolution d'une paroisse suburbaine marseillaise. Le Bon Pasteur. Essai de sociologie religieuse.* Marseilles: Impr. Saint-Léon, 1953. 168 pp.

178. Houtart, F. "Les paroisses de Bruxelles (1803-1951)," *Bulletin de Recherches Econ. et Social,* XVIII (1953), 671-748.
An article based on the historical evolution of the parish body in Brussels.

179. Isambert, A. "Classes sociales et pratique religieuse paroissiales," *Cahiers Int. de Soc.,* XIV (1953), 141-153.

A collection of reflections on a sociological problem of grave pastoral consequences.

180. Houtart, F. "Les paroisses de Chicago et leur importance respective." *Chronique sociale de France*, LXIII (1955) 77-84.

181. Pin, E. *Pratique religieuse et classes sociales dans une paroisse urbaine: Saint-Pothin a Lyón.* Paris: Spes, 1956. 444 pp.
An extraordinary piece of research on a city parish in Lyon which displays a noticeable interest in discovering not only religious practice but the mentality of the people as well.

182. Massion, J. *La Paroisse Sainte-Alix. Ebauche de sociologie religieuse.* Brussels: La Pensée Catholique, 1956. 64 pp.

183. Daniel, Y. *L'Equipement paroissial d'un diocèse urbain: Paris (1802-1956).* Paris: Ed. Oeuvre, 1957. 198 pp.
Despite the work of Le Bras, historical sources were being overlooked in some research. Today this vital field is gaining ground again, as can be seen in this study of Daniel's.

184. Daniel, Y., Le Mouel, G. *Paroisses d'hier . . . Paroisses de demain.* Paris: Grasset, 1957. 264 pp.

185. Winninger, P. *Construir des églises. Les dimensions des paroisses et les contradictions de l'apostolat dans les villes.* Paris: Cerf, 1957. 256 pp.

186. Rica Basagoiti, J. M. de la. *La parroquia de Nuestra Señora de las Mercedes de las Arenas. Estudio de Sociología religiosa.* Bilbao: El Mensajero del Corazón de Jesús, 1957. 154 pp.
This Spanish work opens up a broad horizon to students of religious sociology in Spain.

187. Houtart, F. "Dimensions nouvelles de la paroisse

urbaine," *Nouv. Rev. Théol.*, LXXX (1958), 384-394.

188. Fichter, J. H. *Soziologie der Pfarrgruppen. Untersuchungen zur Struktur und Dynamik der Gruppen einer deutschen Pfarrei.* Münster: Aschendorffsche Verlag, 1958. 178 pp.
This is undoubtedly the best piece of religious sociology ever done on a group of German parishes. The author, the American Jesuit Father Fichter, is a specialist in parish themes.

b) Juridical View

Parish law enjoyed a period of great brilliance before the last war. Recently it has been the Catholic University of America which has made the most contributions to the field.

189. Ernst, H. *Pfarrer und Pfarramt nach dem CIC.* Regensburg: 1932.
190. Fini, L. *Evoluzione storico-canonica della cura d'anime nelle catedrali.* Urbania: 1943.
191. Marmiez, H. *La paroisse d'après le droit canonique.* Fribourg: 1944.
192. Mundy, T. *The Union of Parish.* Washington: 1945.
193. Kelley, B. *The Functions Reserved to Pastors.* Washington: Catholic Univ. of America Press, 1947.
194. Mauro, T. "Appunti sul regime giuridico delle chiese parrocchiali nell diritto italiano," in *Il diritto ecclesiastico.* Milan: 1950.
195. Mickells, A. B. *The Constitutive Elements of Parishes.* Washington: Catholic Univ. of America Press, 1950.
196. González, F. *De parocho religioso eiusque superiores locali.* Washington: 1950.
197. Aguis, L. M. *Summarium iurium et officiorum paro-*

chorum ad normam CIC. Naples: D'Auria, 1953. 258 pp.

198. Fernández Regatillo, E. *Derecho parroquial.* Santander: Sal Terrae, 1953. 618 pp.
199. Muller, F. *De paroichia domui religiose comissa.* Washington: 1956.
200. Noser, H. B. *Pfarrei und Kirchgemeinde. Stude su ihrem rechtlichen Begriff und grundsätzlichen Verhältnis.* Fribourg (Switz.): 1957.
201. Barcia Martin, L. "Potestad parroquial" in the joint work, *La Potestad de la Iglesia.* Barcelona: Flors, 1960. Pp. 99-148.
202. Poggiaspalla, F. *La diócesis y la parroquia.* (Span. trans.) Barcelona: ELE, 1961. 129 pp.
203. Useros, M. "La parroquia, tema de la Ecclesiología y del Derecho Canónico. Notas a un libro," *Rev. Esp. Der. Can.*, XVII (1962), 191-208.

5. Limits of the Parish Apostolate

The subject of the parochial and super-parochial apostolate has furnished material for much discussion, especially in the years before World War II. It would seem that tempers have not completely calmed down even yet, though the growth in importance of the parish is undeniable. But it is still true that the parish alone will not be capable of fulfilling the great task facing the Church. Tradition has already accepted other apostolic paths besides strictly parochial ones.

204. Zimmermann, K. "Ist die Pfarrgemeinde die einzige christliche Gemeinschaftsform?" *Deutsches Volk* (Sept. 1934).
States the problem at the time of the Nazi rise to power.

205. Lardone, G. *Ritorniamo a la Parrocchia.* Turin: L.I.C.E., 1936. 368 pp.
206. Höffner, J. "Um das Pfarrprinzip," *Trierer Theol. Zeitschrift,* LVI (1947), 60-62.
207. Svoboda, R. "Ordentliche und ausserordentliche Seelsorge," *Theol. Prakt. Quart.,* XCIV (1941), 12-20; *Anima,* IV (1949), 9-17.
208. Rahner, K. "Friedliche Erwägungen über das Pfarrprinzip," *Zeitschrift Für Kathol. Theol.,* LXX (1948), 169-198.
An objective statement of the problem.
209. Höffner, J. "Nochmals das Pfarrprinzip," *Trierer Theol. Zeitschr.,* LVII (1948), 236-239.
210. Guzzetti, G. B. "La parrocchia nelle recenti discussioni," *La Scuola Cattolica,* LXXXI (1953), 415-436.
211. Perenna, R. *Innovazioni o rinnovamento della parrocchia?* Como: Cavalleri, 1950. 144 pp.
212. Rahner, K. *Der Pfarrer. Eine Betrachtung.* Vienna: Herder, 1948. 16 pp.
A model of theological meditation on the parish pastor.
213. Rahner, K. "Betrieb und Pfarrei," *Stimmen der Zeit,* CLIII (1953-54), 401-412.
214. Rau, E. "¿Crisis de la parroquia?" *Revista de Teologia,* IV (1954), 33-43.
215. Tabera, A., Bishop of Albacete. "La parroquia y los religiosos," in *Comunidad cristiana parroquial,* (No. 14), 335-396.
216. Spiazzi, R. "Il posto e la funzione del laicato nella Parrocchia," in *Parrocchia,* IX, 153-173.

6. Pontifical Texts on the Parish

There are very few publications that gather together pontifical texts on the parish, making it necessary to turn to collections. Fortunately, the latter are rather plentiful; we have not cited them because they are widely familiar.

217. "Tu parroquia y tu pastor." Documents and themes for the celebration of Parish Day. Ed. by the National Board of Spanish Catholic Action. Madrid: 1944. 159 pp.
This edition is now outmoded, but it still contains some worthwhile texts.
218. Dander, F. X. "Papsworte über die Pfarre," in *Die Pfarre* (No. 26), 9-14.
A selection of a few papal texts.
219. Hombría, A. "La parroquia en el Magisterio de la Iglesia," in *Comunidad cristiana parroquial* (No. 14), 47-86.
220. *La Parroquia según Pio XII y Juan XXIII*. Madrid: Editorial A.C.E., 1960. 80 pp.

7. Other Aspects of the Parish

221. Fanfani, A. "Parroci e servizio sociale," in *Riv. Clero Italiano,* XXXI (1950), 266-87.
222. Esteban Romero, A. A. *El estado mayor del párroco* (2nd ed., 1961). Madrid: Euramérica. 242 pp.
223. Azagra, J. "El problema económica," in *Comunidad cristiana parroquial* (No. 14), 415-458.
A study of the different solutions to the problem of the parish's economic support.
224. Montero, A. "Parroquias piloto en España," in *Comunidad cristiana parroquial* (No. 14), 533-565.
A rapid and optimistic tour of a few vital Spanish parishes selected at random from different regions of the country.
225. Arnaboldi, P. M. *Al servicio de la pastoral parroquial,* Valencia: Ed. FAC, 1959. 200 pp.

An explanation of the FAC Movement as applied to the parish.

226. *La parroquia al contraataque, El censo parroquial* and *El FAC en las parroquias pequeñas*, Alfara del Patriarca, Valencia: FAC Publications.
These three brief volumes offer practical suggestions for revitalizing parishes.

227. "Paroisse et catéchèse," *Lumen Vitae*, XIV (1959)

228. Garail, M. *La Famille et la Paroisse. Les perspectives d'une Pastorale Moderne*. Paris: Association du Mariage Chrétien, 1961. 150 pp.

229. "Paroisse et Catéchèse des Enfants," special issue of *Catéchèse* (Oct. 1961), pp. 475-602.

230. Morel, B. "L'Oecumenisme au plan paroissial," in *Découverte de l'Oecumenisme*. Bruges: Desclée de Br., 1962, pp. 144-158.